Do You Really Know

American English?

Do You Really Know
American English?

How Truly
American
Are You?

William C. Harvey, M.S.

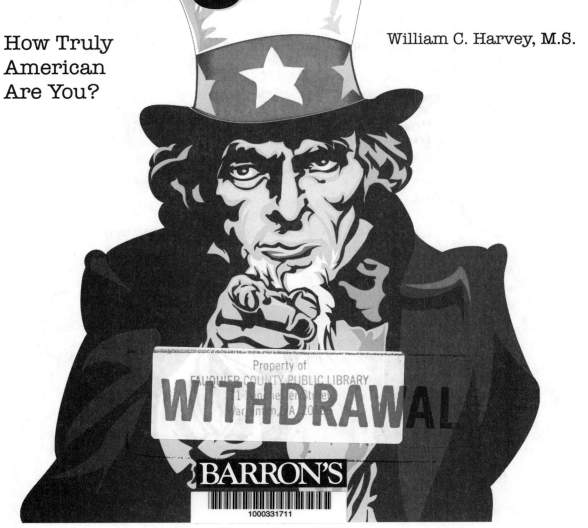

BARRON'S

To my folks, Roger and Pat Harvey

About the Author
William C. Harvey is founder of Language Services Institute, a highly successful linguistic program aimed specifically at meeting the needs of today's busy adult learner. He has received the "Project of the Year Award" from Cal State University, Fullerton, for his work in ESL curriculum development, and has traveled extensively throughout the West Coast giving workshops and seminars to teachers and professional organizations. Bill has written several books for Barron's, all of which enjoy a well-deserved popularity.

© Copyright 2005 by William C. Harvey
Illustrations © Copyright 2005 by Barron's Educational Series, Inc.

All inquiries should be addressed to:
Barron's Educational Series, Inc.
250 Wireless Boulevard
Hauppauge, New York 11788
http://www.barronseduc.com

International Standard Book Number 0-7641-2882-5

Library of Congress Control Number 2004047671

Library of Congress Cataloging-in-Publication Data
Harvey, William C.
    Do You Really Know American English?: How Truly American Are You? / William C. Harvey.
        p. cm.
    ISBN 0-7641-2882-5 (alk. paper)
    1. English language—Spoken English—United States—Problems, exercises, etc. 2. English language—United States—Problems, exercises, etc. 3. Figures of speech—Problems, exercises, etc. 4. Americanisms—Problems, exercises, etc. I. Title.

PE2808.8H37   2004
428.3—dc22   2004047671

Printed in the United States of America
9 8 7 6 5 4 3 2 1

CONTENTS

CHAPTER ONE: THE SIMPLE LIFE / 1
    I.   We, the People! / 2
    II. What'd You Call Me? / 7
    III. Nice Body! / 14
    IV. Let's Eat! / 22
    V.   Animal Lover! / 29

CHAPTER TWO: SPECIAL DETAIL / 39
    VI. All Kinds of Stuff! / 40
    VII. Bits and Pieces! / 46
    VIII. Tell Me About It! / 51
    IX. Tell Me Where! / 63
    X.   Say When! / 69

CHAPTER THREE: SMALL TALK / 77
    XI. Pick a Number! / 78
    XII. Take a Letter! / 82
    XIII. And? / 88
    XIV. Chit-Chat! / 93
    XV. Just Do It! / 98

CHAPTER FOUR: A LOT GOING ON / 103
    XVI. Need Some Action? / 104
    XVII. Acting Strange! / 110
    XVIII. Vicious Verbs! / 116
    XIX. Playing Around! / 122
    XX. Kid's Stuff! / 127

CHAPTER FIVE: MIGHTY MESSAGES / 135
    XXI. Mom Used to Say! / 136
    XXII. The Religious Past! / 142
    XXIII. Express Yourself! / 148
    XXIV. Wacky Words! / 154
    XXV. Foreign Imports! / 157

CHAPTER SIX: THAT'S ENTERTAINMENT / 166

XXVI. Film Fest! / 167
XXVII. Song and Dance! / 172
XXVIII. What a Laugh! / 180
XXIX. Fame! / 187
XXX. In the News! / 194

CHAPTER SEVEN: THE GOOD OLD DAYS / 201

XXXI. Duty Calls! / 202
XXXII. Wild West! / 208
XXXIII. Old English! / 214
XXXIV. Since the Sixties! / 221
XXXV. More, More, More! / 229

INTRODUCTION

It's amazing. Wherever you go in the world, you can always recognize American English, because the language has a distinctive sound that is truly all its own. What makes it so unique is the fact that it is packed with words and expressions that only Americans understand.

On the following pages, I have tried to capture the true spirit of our national language by formulating categorized lists of words, phrases, and expressions that reflect the speech of our nation. Such a collection does not need to be studied formally and can quickly be acquired by completing the word game activities.

The instructions are simple—complete each activity at your own pace, check your answers, and write down the number of points you got. At the end of the chapter go to **"What's My Score?"** and indicate your total score. A Grand Total appears at the end of the last chapter. Before you know it, you too will be speaking all-American English!

Before You Begin

The chapters consist of several game-like activities, with the answers provided at the end of each cluster. Words and phrases are divided into easy-to-follow categories, so that readers can move through the book any way they choose. Moreover, icons indicate these specialized selections:

A LITTLE HISTORY
Gives background information on certain key expressions, including word origins.

BORN IN THE U.S.A.
Offers insights into culture, traditions, or trends that remain consistent all across America today.

ON YOUR OWN
Challenges the readers to handle all-American words and expressions without assistance. If they fail, only encyclopedias or the Internet can save them!

WORDS OF WISDOM
Provides witty, insightful quotes from famous people in U.S. history.

SAY IT RIGHT
Gives tips on structure, usage, or in some cases pronunciation of certain words and phrases.

WHAT'S MY SCORE?
Allows readers to assess their knowledge by comparing the total number of their correct answers with the total number of possible answers. This icon appears once, at the end of each chapter.

Chapter One

The Simple Life

I. WE, THE PEOPLE!

Q1. What better way to begin than by talking about the American people themselves. Match each word with the CLOSEST meaning:

1.	dame	a.	bambino
2.	chum	b.	groom
3.	lad	c.	the missus
4.	pop	d.	fella
5.	better half	e.	adolescent
6.	old maid	f.	lass
7.	guy	g.	spinster
8.	folks	h.	sonny
9.	tot	i.	dad
10.	missy	j.	pal
11.	hubby	k.	gal
12.	teenybopper	l.	kin

Q2. Join the words that belong together. Do any look familiar?

1.	mother	a.	clock
2.	son	b.	brother
3.	grandfather	c.	prodigal
4.	father	d.	time
5.	frat	e.	nature

Q3. Now fill in the blanks:

1. I wish I had a fairy _____ .   a. lady
2. He acted like a perfect _____ on our date.   b. sister
3. We read stories about _____ Remus.   c. godmother
4. Mom was a pom-pom _____ in high school.   d. woman
5. He was truly a man's _____.   e. gentleman
6. That guy is an excellent _____ figure.   f. boy
7. What do they say about the scorn of a _____ ?   g. uncle
8. I'll need _____ luck at the card game.   h. man
9. My kid _____ always gets in my hair.   i. father
10. Boy oh _____ !   j. girl

Answers

Q1. 1. k   2. j   3. h   4. i   5. c   6. g   7. d   8. l   9. a   10. f
       11. b   12. e
Q2. 1. e   2. c   3. a   4. d   5. b
Q3. 1. c   2. e   3. g   4. j   5. h   6. i   7. d   8. a   9. b   10. f

Give yourself 1 point for every correct answer: _____

BORN IN THE U.S.A.

- Men have nearly always taken the lead roles in American society, so one-liners about the male sex abound:

  *The job today **separated the men from the boys.**
  By the way, I'm **going out with the boys tonight.**
  Don't wait up, because **boys will be boys!***

- Americans label their parents differently, from **mom and dad** to **ma and pa.** They do the same thing with other family members:

  *I love my **sis, granny, gramps, auntie,** and **cuz!***

ON YOUR OWN

1. *How did you become a **friend indeed**?*
2. *Have you ever met a **son of a gun**?*

A LITTLE HISTORY

- The Puritans in the seventeenth century believed that marriages consisted of two halves—the body and the soul. The soul, which was reflected in the wife's behavior, was therefore considered the **better half.**
- **Grandfather clock** came from a popular song of the 1880s that began, ***My grandfather's clock was too tall for the shelf, so it stood ninety years on the floor...***
- During the late nineteenth century, American author Joel Chandler Harris began to introduce the ***dialect tales*** of **Uncle Remus,** an old slave from the south. Based on true stories, Harris focused on the age-old wisdom that allowed slaves to cleverly outwit their masters. For over a century, his poems, stories, and proverbs have brought enjoyment to millions of readers worldwide.

Q4. How about people's names? Pick the correct word from the other column:

1.	Heavens to …	___	a.	Mike
2.	Dear … letter	___	b.	Johnny
3.	Whoa, …	___	c.	Bobby
4.	For the love of …!	___	d.	John
5.	Raggedy …	___	e.	Jack
6.	Uncle …	___	f.	Nelly
7.	Every Tom, Dick, and …	___	g.	Betsy
8.	… of all trades	___	h.	Thomas
9.	… come lately	___	i.	Charlie
10.	… horse	___	j.	Harry
11.	Doubting …	___	k.	Sam
12.	… pins	___	l.	Anne

Q5. Make these connections:

1. Joe		a. Reb
2. Geez		b. Tom
3. The real		c. Susan
4. Life of		d. Ruth
5. Johnny		e. Cain
6. Jumping		f. Mary
7. Peeping		g. Jane
8. Baby		h. McCoy
9. Lazy		i. Jack
10. Bloody		j. Louise
11. Calamity		k. Blow
12. Raising		l. Riley

Bury the hatchet

Q6. Choose the right name from the list below:

1. He's just another average _____.
2. Faster than you can say _____ Robinson.
3. That's a real _____ Dandy.
4. The kids love _____ Goat's Gruff.
5. I think we're all even _____.
6. Big _____ is in London, England.
7. Please put your _____ Hancock right here.
8. What the _____ Hill are you doing?
9. Somebody here is a real _____ Arnold.
10. Is Kris Kringle the same guy as St. _____?

Fred	Mark
Benedict	Paul
Ben	Joe
Adam	John
Jack	David
Randy	Sam
Earl	Nick
Billy	Jim
Bobby	Luke
Steven	George

Q7. Fill in the blanks to complete more well-known expressions:

1. Like _____, like son.
2. Don't throw the _____ out with the bath water.
3. He made me cry, _____.
4. I'm the low _____ on the totem pole.
5. For him, it was just _____ play.
6. That's an old _____ tale.
7. We'll handle it with _____ gloves.
8. He's only a fair-weather _____.
9. Will you be my pen _____?
10. Necessity is the _____ of invention.

a. kid
b. mother
c. father
d. friend
e. wives'
f. baby
g. pal
h. man
i. uncle
j. child's

Answers

Q4. 1. g 2. d 3. f 4. a 5. l 6. k 7. j 8. e 9. b 10. i
       11. h 12. c

Q5. 1. k 2. j 3. h 4. l 5. a 6. i 7. b 8. d 9. c 10. f
       11. g 12. e

Q6. 1. Joe 2. Jack 3. Jim 4. Billy 5. Steven 6. Ben 7. John
       8. Sam 9. Benedict 10. Nick

Q7. 1. c 2. f 3. i 4. h 5. j 6. e 7. a 8. d 9. g 10. b

Give yourself 1 point for every correct answer:

ON YOUR OWN

1. *Touch your **Adam's apple**.*
2. *How are **up the hill** and **the beanstalk** related?*
3. *Will you ever rob **Peter** to pay **Paul**?*
4. *You are **in like** whom?*
5. *What color is your **john**?*

A LITTLE HISTORY

- The original goateed **Uncle Sam** was Samuel Wilson, a merchant who sold beef and pork to the U.S. Army during the War of 1812. Because the barrels were marked **U.S.**, soldiers jokingly began to call their meals **gifts from Uncle Sam**.

- The first **peeping Tom** was Tom, the tailor, who tried to look at Lady Godiva as she rode naked through the streets of Coventry. Perhaps as a warning to future peeping Toms, according to the story, he was struck blind.

- The Greek philosopher, Plato, was the first to use the expression **old wives' tale**, but it was the Dutch in the 1300s who claimed that certain superstitions came from the gossip of local elderly women. Today, we use the phrase to describe any information that is based on rumor or hearsay.

BORN IN THE U.S.A.

- Two of the most common names in American English are **Jack** (*Jack-o-lantern, jackhammer, jackpot, Jack Frost, jack cheese, jack-in-the-box, jackknife*) and its twin, **John** (*John Doe, Johnny come lately, John Q. Public*).
- The use of proper names is still an all-American trend today:

  *While checking out the **Dow Jones** on **Wall Street**, I poured a little **Jack Daniels** in my cup of **Joe**.*
  *We fought hard trying **to keep up with the Joneses**.*

WORDS OF WISDOM

"A son is a son till he gets him a wife, but a daughter's a daughter for the rest of your life."

Anonymous

II. WHAT'D YOU CALL ME?

Blind as a bat

Q8. Without a doubt, Americans lead the world in name-calling. Look at these words that have been used for years when referring to a person whose intelligence was in question. You'll need to unscramble some letters first.

1.	etosgo	otidi	<u>stooge</u>	<u>idiot</u>
2.	peod	bahueddm	____	____
3.	wiidtm	lofo	____	____
4.	anibrrbdi	ttwiin	____	____
5.	naggidnil	ornmo	____	____

6. lieonptsm   pitsdu   _____   _____
7. cajsask   lebmuldb   _____   _____
8. moppinonco   ahpnide   _____   _____
9. eanmilrab   oodd   _____   _____
10. obbo   kublnlmus   _____   _____
11. adathef   ftilhaw   _____   _____
12. told   mydmu   _____   _____

Q9. Americans also talk a lot about folks who act a little strange. Circle five words in each line that refer to a **kook** or a **screwball**:

1. emamadamlocopsyholpsychooypsamrayzarcrazyrazypsts-nunutssatamopox
2. wharcdoowhackoojoolloonyynouttaabbattyyttdayaffdaffyoy-cokcuckooche
3. dabonkerskersoypoloopypsycracrackedopiennopinsanenylool-goffogoofyo

Keep going, but all these need is the missing word:

4. He's _____ his marbles.
5. He's got a _____ loose.
6. He's out of his _____.
7. He's off his _____.
8. He's not playing with a _____ deck.
9. He's a basket _____.
10. He has his lights on, but nobody's _____.

Q10. Now, choose the appropriate name-calling word to complete each sentence below:

1. He's a squirt; a …   ____   a. hobo
2. She's a blabbermouth, a …   ____   b. floozy
3. I'm a wisecracker, a …   ____   c. fuddy-duddy
4. You're a hoodlum, a …   ____   d. lug
5. He's an old fogey, a …   ____   e. brat
6. You're a blockhead, a …   ____   f. tattletale
7. She's a hussy, a …   ____   g. lazy bones
8. He's a pill, a …   ____   h. battleaxe

9. I'm a sucker, a ...   ____   i. sap
10. He's an old tramp, a ...   ____   j. pipsqueak
11. She's an old hag, a ...   ____   k. smart Alec
12. You're a loafer, a ...   ____   l. crook

Answers

Q8. 2. dope, dumbhead   3. dimwit, fool   4. birdbrain, nitwit
     5. dingaling, moron   6. simpleton, stupid   7. jackass, dumbbell
     8. nincompoop, pinhead   9. lamebrain, dodo
     10. boob, numbskull   11. fathead, halfwit   12. dolt, dummy

Q9. 1. mad, loco, psycho, crazy, nuts
     2. whacko, loony, batty, daffy, cuckoo
     3. bonkers, loopy, cracked, insane, goofy
     4. lost, losing   5. screw   6. mind, gourd   7. rocker   8. full
     9. case   10. home

Q10. 1. j   2. f   3. k.   4. l   5. c   6. d   7. b   8. e   9. i   10. a
     11. h   12. g

Give yourself 1 point for every correct answer:

A LITTLE HISTORY

- As industry grew in the U.S., new machines began to fill the home
  and workplace. Many would fall apart due to poor construction,
  often resulting in strange sounds and behavior. As a result, individu-
  als exhibiting abnormal human behavior were told they too had a
  screw loose.
- **Fogey** comes from the word **foggy**, which was once a disrespect-
  ful name in Scotland for an older man who was **behind the times**.
- The word **loony** is linked to the loon, a bird with a strange cry
  that sounds like the laugh of an insane person. It is also a shorter
  way of saying the word **lunatic**. Today it is used to describe any
  crazy or unusual behavior.
- The word **bigwig** refers to a person of influence or wealth. In
  the eighteenth century men of importance wore white wigs in
  America and Europe. In Great Britain, some men in the legal field
  still wear them.

Hitch one's
wagon to a star

BORN IN THE U.S.A.

- Calling other people nicknames is a tradition practiced worldwide. And so it is in the U.S., where lots of folks go through life with monikers like *Bubba*, *Shorty*, *Kitty*, and *Pops*.

SAY IT RIGHT

- As you read through this book, you may run across a few expressions that are presented more than once. That's because they fit into more than one category, or are a little more common than the rest.

WORDS OF WISDOM

"Associate yourself with men of good quality if you esteem your own reputation; for 'tis better to be alone than in bad company."

George Washington

ON YOUR OWN

1. *Have you ever met an **angler** or a **grease monkey**?*
2. *Do you know any **nannies** or **brownies**?*
3. *When were you a **bundle of joy**?*

Q11. Keep going, just fill in the missing word:

1. She frets about everything. She's a worry _____.	a. wallflower
2. Look at that bruiser! What a ____!	b. ham
3. Did you hear about Dr. Smith? I think he's a _____.	c. wart
4. Don't be a ____ . Jump!	d. hog
5. He never says anything at parties. He's a ____.	e. honcho
6. After I said it, I felt like a _____.	f. thug
7. Get out of my way, you road ____!	g. cookie
8. Look at her play! She's one tough _____.	h. heel
9. Are you the head _____ around here?	i. sissy
10. Did you see her act? What a _____!	j. quack

Q12. Find the BEST definition:

1. A southpaw is …	a. strong
2. A shyster is …	b. temperamental
3. A rubberneck is …	c. prissy
4. A knockout is …	d. left-handed
5. A prima donna is …	e. young
6. A hotshot is …	f. curious
7. A square is …	g. boring
8. A he-man is …	h. dishonest
9. A butterfingers is …	i. talkative
10. A whippersnapper is …	j. clumsy
11. A windbag is …	k. self-assured
12. A prude is …	l. beautiful

Q13. Keep up the name-calling:

1. A rookie is …	a. a dawdler
2. A pantywaist is …	b. a meddler
3. A geezer is …	c. a rat
4. A slowpoke is …	d. a novice
5. A lush is …	e. a rowdy
6. A con is …	f. a wimp
7. A moocher is …	g. a stick-in-the-mud
8. A buttinski is …	h. a hick
9. A hillbilly is …	i. a beggar
10. A squealer is …	j. an alky
11. A wet blanket is …	k. an old buzzard
12. A roughneck is …	l. a jailbird

Q14. Here are more words to match:

1. yahoo	a. freak
2. bombshell	b. boy scout
3. whiz kid	c. bore
4. greenhorn	d. rail
5. beanpole	e. yokel
6. brat	f. half-pint
7. weirdo	g. tenderfoot
8. drip	h. brain
9. pee wee	i. fox
10. goody-goody	j. little monster

Answers

Q11. 1. c   2. f   3. j   4. i   5. a   6. h   7. d   8. g   9. e   10. b

Q12. 1. d   2. h   3. f   4. l   5. b   6. k   7. g   8. a   9. j   10. e
      11. i   12. c

Q13. 1. d   2. f   3. k   4. a   5. j   6. l   7. i   8. b   9. h   10. c
      11. g   12. e

Q14. 1. e   2. i   3. h   4. g   5. d   6. j   7. a   8. c   9. f   10. b

Give yourself 1 point for every correct answer:

ON YOUR OWN

1. *Do like **back seat drivers** or **fair-weather friends**?*
2. *Name a **blowhard** and a **teetotaler**.*
3. *Would you like to be a **gold digger** or a **teacher's pet**?*

A LITTLE HISTORY

- A **stooge** was originally a theatrical term referring to a comedian's accomplice hidden in the audience. Since he or she was often the target of pranks or ridicule, a stooge gradually became synonymous with **fool**.

- **Thug** comes from the foreign word for cheat or swindler. The original thugs were members of an organization of guerilla fighters in India.

- **Quack** is short for the Dutch word *quacksalver*, or one who quacks loudly (like a duck) about his medicinal salves.

- Years ago, Native Americans on the move would put out their fires with blankets that were soaked in a local creek or river. Similarly, a person who is a **wet blanket** is a spoilsport and pessimist, extinguishing the enthusiasm of anyone nearby.

Quack

BORN IN THE U.S.A.

- A person in a position of leadership is often referred to as the *chief* or *head honcho*, the *top dog* or *top banana*, or the *big cheese*, *big Kahuna*, or *big wheel*. Similarly, anyone of great wealth, fame, or influence is considered a *fat cat*, a *bigwig*, or a *big shot*.

- For years, the bad boy in the neighborhood has been labeled a *rotten egg*, a *louse*, a *scoundrel*, a *cad*, a *bum*, a *rascal*, a *creep*, or a *jerk*. If he was exceptionally cruel, words like *meany*, *bully*, or *tough guy* were used. A mere *troublemaker* was simply a *rabble-rouser* or occasional *pain in the neck*.
- To keep up with the times, most men in the U.S. have learned that words like *chick*, *broad*, or *dame* are no longer used in reference to females.

SAY IT RIGHT

- Many name-calling words are actually two or more words in one: You're nothing but a **busybody**, a **crybaby**, and a **know-it-all**!
- Here are some longer ones: You're a **diamond in the rough**, I'm a **glutton for punishment**, and she's a **babe in the woods**!

WORDS OF WISDOM

"The Lord prefers common-looking people. That is why He made so many of them."

Abraham Lincoln

III. NICE BODY!

Q15. In any language, parts of the human body have been used to make a point. Let's see how many of the following expressions can you finish:

1. You're a sight for sore _____.
2. I've got a frog in my _____.
3. It looks like he really took it on the _____ .
4. Stay out of trouble; keep your _____ clean.
5. He saw her beauty, and got swept off his _____.
6. We worked our _____ to the bone.
7. Say that again, and I'll give you a _____ sandwich.
8. Let's go; shake a _____.

9. Thanks for sticking your _____ out for me.
10. Great job! Give him a _____.
11. Hang in there, and keep a stiff upper _____.
12. Cat got your _____?
13. He's got quite a chip on his _____.
14. I'm always breaking things; I'm all _____.
15. Tell me what happened; I'm all _____.
16. I'm nervous, I've got butterflies in my _____.
17. She's sensitive; she wears her _____ on her sleeve.
18. Leave me alone; get off my _____.
19. I can tell; it's written all over your _____.
20. Let's talk; I need to get something off my _____.
21. I don't know; I haven't seen hide or _____ of him.
22. Two _____ are better than one.
23. What it needs is a little _____ grease.
24. They were fighting _____ and nail.
25. You bother me; you really get under my _____.

Q16. Now, find the words that are CLOSEST in meaning:

1. Mitts	_____	Knees	Heart
2. Noggin	_____	Fanny	Arms
3. Peepers	_____	Teeth	Guts
4. Locks	_____	Brain	Neck
5. Ticker	_____	Navel	Hands
6. Can	_____	Nose	Elbows
7. Tootsies	_____	Bones	Eyes
8. Puss	_____	Ears	Toes
9. Gizzards	_____	Hair	Cheek
10. Honker	_____	Shins	Mouth

Cry over spilled milk

Q17. Join letters from these two columns to create new expressions, and then put their combination next to the appropriate sentence below:

a.	funny	a.	shoulder
b.	yellow	b.	knee
c.	shut	c.	foot
d.	pin	d.	bone
e.	pinky	e.	belly
f.	forked	f.	arm
g.	trick	g.	skin
h.	last	h.	tongue
i.	cold	i.	eye
j.	thin	j.	head
k.	strong	k.	legs
l.	hot	l.	finger

1. I'm exhausted; I need some … before I go back to work.
2. He's a coward, a … .
3. It feels weird whenever I hit my … .
4. This hand has a swollen … .
5. Don't tell her the bad news; she has … .
6. Sorry, but I can't run with this … .
7. He's a liar, and speaks with a … .
8. To get control, they like to … their victims.
9. The guy's a jerk, a real … .
10. I ignored her, and gave her the … .
11. My car is on its … .
12. I gave him a … as a practical joke.

Answers

Q15. 1. eyes   2. throat   3. chin   4. nose   5. feet   6. fingers
7. knuckle   8. leg   9. neck   10. hand   11. lip   12. tongue
13. shoulder   14. thumbs   15. ears   16. stomach   17. heart
18. back   19. face   20. chest   21. hair   22. heads   23. elbow
24. tooth   25. skin

Q16. 1. hands 2. brain 3. eyes 4. hair 5. heart 6. fanny
7. toes 8. mouth 9. guts 10. nose

Q17. 1. c-i 2. b-e 3. a-d 4. e-l 5. j-g 6. g-b 7. f-h 8. k-f 9. d-j
10. i-a 11. h-k 12. l-c

Give yourself 1 point for every correct answer:

SAY IT RIGHT

- Listen for combinations of body parts in the same expression:

  *She stood **head** and **shoulders** above the rest.*
  *He **thumbed** his **nose** at my idea.*
  *It cost me an **arm** and a **leg**.*

BORN IN THE U.S.A.

The word **belly** refers to the underside of almost anything in American English, but is generally used to mean the abdomen. Check out these other expressions:

  *Don't **bellyache** if you burn your **beer belly** on the **potbelly** stove.*
  *He did a **belly flop** and landed on his **belly button**.*
  *Her company didn't go **belly up**, so she let out a big **belly laugh**.*

ON YOUR OWN

1. *Point to your **bean**, **noodle**, or **gourd**.*
2. *Scratch your **bum**, **keister**, or **toosh**.*
3. *Touch your **schnozzle**, **snout**, or **bazoo**.*
4. *Do you have **crow's feet**?*
5. *Open your **yap** or **trap**.*

A LITTLE HISTORY

- These references to the skeleton come from Europe, and have been around for centuries:

  *He's nothing but **skin** and **bones**.*
  *You need to **bone** up on your history.*
  *I've got a **bone** to pick with you!*
  *Make no **bones** about it.*

- **Elbow grease** is a slang expression from the late seventeenth century meaning sweaty, hard work, and it once related to the polishing of wooden furniture. Today it refers to any strenuous physical effort or exertion.
- In the 1800s, a boy would challenge another to knock a chip of wood off his shoulder in order to start a fight. Today, anyone with a **chip on his shoulder** is a bit touchy, and always on the prowl for an argument.

Q18. Can you come up with one classic expression for each of these sets of cue words? (Hint: Don't let the word order fool you!)

1. ears/wet   <u>**He's a little wet behind the ears.**</u>
2. lips/sink   _____
3. mouth/foot   _____
4. heart/stomach   _____
5. hair/chest   _____
6. eye/meets   _____
7. heart/home   _____
8. ear/other   _____
9. money/mouth   _____
10. finger/wrapped   _____
11. hip/shoot   _____
12. eyes/wool   _____
13. ears/music   _____
14. grave/foot   _____
15. foot/shoe   _____

Q19. Well then! Answer these important questions:

1. **What** are you the apple of?
2. It's the rule of **what**?
3. **What** do you cross for good luck?
4. Put my best **what** forward?
5. It's a shot in the **what**?
6. You're pulling my **what**?
7. It's a slip of the **what**?
8. **What** is he cooling and dragging?
9. You learned it by **what**?
10. **What** should you bite for saying that?

a. arm
b. fingers
c. heart
d. heels
e. lip
f. tongue
g. foot
h. eye
i. thumb
j. leg

Q20. How quickly can you fill these in with body parts?

1. Butter   _____
2. Private   _____
3. Green   _____
4. Rubber   _____
5. Twinkle   _____

Keep going, but in these common one-liners, the same word is repeated:

6. Sharing **heart** to **heart**
7. Dancing _____ to _____
8. Meeting _____ to _____
9. Boxing _____ to _____
10. Seeing _____ to _____
11. Racing _____ to _____
12. Dueling _____ to _____

Put your money where your mouth is

Q21. Fill in the blanks with the same body part twice:

1. It was a sight for sore _____. I couldn't believe my _____.
2. She really let her _____ down. They always get in my _____.
3. I can't put my _____ on it. He didn't lay a _____ on her.
4. We got to rub _____ with them. I need a little _____ room.

5. They paid through the _____. She turned up her _____ at me.
6. Let's find a way to save _____. He really had egg on his _____.
7. I finally got my _____ in the door. We had to put our _____ down.
8. We'll just play it by _____. Keep your _____ to the ground.
9. Never bite the _____ that feeds you. I wash my _____ of it.
10. That was way over my _____. You've got a good _____ on your shoulders.

Answers

Q18. 2. Loose lips sink ships.
3. I put my foot in my mouth.
4. The way to a man's heart is through his stomach.
5. It'll put hair on your chest.
6. There's more than meets the eye.
7. Home is where your heart is.
8. It goes in one ear and out the other.
9. Put your money where your mouth is.
10. She's got you wrapped around her little finger.
11. He shoots from the hip.
12. Don't let him pull the wool over your eyes.
13. That's music to my ears.
14. He's got one foot in the grave.
15. The shoe's on the other foot.

Q19. 1. h   2. i   3. b   4. g   5. a   6. j   7. e   8. d   9. c   10. f

Q20. 1. fingers   2. eye   3. thumb   4. neck   5. toes   6. heart
7. cheek   8. face   9. toe   10. eye   11. neck   12. back

Q21. 1. eyes   2. hair   3. finger   4. elbows   5. nose   6. face
7. foot   8. ear   9. hand   10. head

Give yourself 1 point for every correct answer:

BORN IN THE U.S.A.

• Notice how often American English aims at the brain or head:

> *My sore**head** scatter**brained** boss has **brain**washed us to always get a **head** start on our **brain**storming sessions.*

• The hand is another popular body part:

> *On the other **hand**, I've got to **hand** it to you. Your **hands** are tied and you've got your **hands** full. I know you like the back of my **hand**! I couldn't tell you off **hand**, but if the **hand** is quicker than the eye, your **hand** has been in the cookie jar; so **hand** it over!*

A LITTLE HISTORY

• To **pull one's leg** originally meant to cheat or trick another person, or to **trip one up** for personal gain. It is now used to mean a harmless joke or kidding around.
• **Washing one's hands** of something comes from the biblical story of Pontius Pilate, the Roman official who refused to take responsibility for the execution of Jesus. Today, it simply means that you don't want to be involved any further.
• As immigrants moved into Native American territory, wars erupted. Sometimes the only way to tell if the enemy was coming was to **put your ear to the ground** and listen for the sound of horses. The expression today refers to being aware of things that might determine the future.

To lose one's marbles

ON YOUR OWN

1. *Move your **pointer**, **middle**, and **ring**.*
2. *Have you ever **cut off your nose to spite your face**?*
3. *Do you know how to **bat your lashes**?*

WORDS OF WISDOM

"Always be a first-rate person of yourself, instead of a second-rate person of somebody else."

Judy Garland

IV. LET'S EAT!

Q22. Read each set of words, and then name the food category:

1. tuna salad, baloney, grilled cheese   ____   a. soups
2. lemon meringue, huckleberry, banana cream ____   b. cookies
3. shredded wheat, oatmeal, corn flakes   ____   c. eggs
4. French, Italian, blue cheese   ____   d. sandwiches
5. sourdough, pumpernickel, rye   ____   e. steaks
6. Roquefort, Swiss, provolone   ____   f. pizzas
7. porterhouse, sirloin, New York   ____   g. dressings
8. popcorn, peanuts, pretzels   ____   h. snacks
9. pepperoni, sausage, cheese   ____   i. potatoes
10. split pea, chicken noodle, French onion   ____   j. donuts
11. Caesar's, chef, cob   ____   k. breads
12. scalloped, mashed, baked   ____   l. pies
13. s'mores, oatmeal, chocolate chip   ____   m. cheeses
14. crumb cake, glazed, sprinkled   ____   n. cereals
15. poached, deviled, sunny-side-up   ____   o. salads

Q23. With the following **vittles**, you'll need to fill in the missing words:

1. black-eyed _____ and hominy _____
2. barbecued spare _____
3. sloppy _____
4. buttermilk _____ with maple _____
5. tapioca _____
6. _____ jerky
7. honey-glazed _____
8. strawberry short _____
9. chicken-fried _____
10. Cornish _____

Answers

Q22. 1. d   2. l   3. n   4. g   5. k   6. m   7. e   8. h   9. f   10. a
    11. o   12. i   13. b   14. j   15. c

Q23. 1. peas, grits   2. ribs   3. joe's   4. pancakes, syrup   5. pudding
    6. beef   7. ham   8. cake   9. steak   10. hen

Give yourself 1 point for every correct answer:

BORN IN THE U.S.A.

- Whether with a smile (***sugar plum, lamb chop, sweetie pie***), or without (***crumb, chicken liver, tub of lard***), Americans enjoy referring to each other as food items. Actually, as a culture, we're obsessed with eating—we yell ***baloney!*** when we think someone's lying, say ***cheese*** in front of cameras, and call our money ***bread***. We even ***eat our words*** when we make a prediction that doesn't come true! Talking about food is as American as … ***mom's apple pie***.

- Salt is a necessary food item in most cultures, and that's why so many American expressions refer to it:

    *As the **salt** of the earth who is truly worth his **salt**, he always takes these things with a grain of **salt**.*

SAY IT RIGHT

- From **gingerbread men** to **fortune cookies**, from **apple turnovers** to **upside down cakes**, and from **cream puffs** to **flap jacks**, Americans are famous for creating descriptive titles for any food item.

ON YOUR OWN

1. *Do you say **po'boys** or **hogies?***
2. *Name something that's in **apple-pie order**.*
3. *Have you ever tried **rocky road, vanilla**, and **Neapolitan** all together?*

WORDS OF WISDOM

"Cauliflower is nothing but cabbage with a college education."

Mark Twain

Q24. Everybody loves sweets. Fill in the blanks to discover some of
America's favorites:

1. S_L_W_T_R T_F_Y
2. B_A_K L_C_R_C_
3. C_N_Y C_N_S
4. B_B_L_ G_M
5. G_M D_O_S
6. C_T_O_ C_N_Y
7. C_A_K_R J_C_S
8. J_L_Y B_A_S
9. J_W B_E_K_R_
10. C_R_M_L C_R_
11. P_A_U_ B_I_T_E
12. B_T_E_S_O_C_ T_F_E_

Q25. Can you guess which words are missing? These are well-known
expressions that refer to foods:

1. Don't cry over spilt _____.
2. I'm in trouble. My _____ is cooked.
3. The proof is in the _____.
4. It didn't amount to a hill of _____.
5. Waiter! There's a fly in my _____.
6. You can't have your _____ and eat it, too.
7. I'm embarrassed. I've got _____ on my face.
8. An _____ a day keeps the doctor away.
9. He's the _____ of the crop.
10. They're inseparable—like two _____ in a pod.
11. She sure is difficult. She's a tough _____ to crack.
12. Polly, want a _____?
13. Say that again, and I'll give you a knuckle _____!
14. Don't listen to him—it's just sour _____.
15. He was wrong, so now he has to eat humble _____.

16. If she doesn't get here soon, I'll go _____.
17. That's really not my cup of _____.
18. They don't pay me much. I make _____.
19. Oh, well, that's the way the _____ crumbles.
20. One _____, two _____, three _____, four.

Q26. Have you ever sampled any of these? Select the BEST match:

1. Greek _____   a. toast
2. Polish _____   b. whiskey
3. Danish _____   c. meatballs
4. Swiss _____   d. salad
5. French _____   e. chocolate cake
6. Swedish _____   f. cheese
7. English _____   g. rice
8. Irish _____   h. sausage
9. Spanish _____   i. tea
10. German _____   j. pastry

And what about dining state to state?

11. Florida   a. beef
12. Wisconsin   b. cheesecake
13. New England   c. apples
14. Nebraska   d. orange juice
15. Idaho   e. lobster
16. Hawaii   f. cheese
17. New York   g. chowder
18. Washington   h. corn
19. Texas   i. potatoes
20. Maine   j. pineapple

Bite the hand that feeds you

Q27. Some name brands in the U.S. are synonymous with certain foods.
Fill in the blanks:

1. Dad's Old-fashioned _____
2. Gerber's _____
3. Hostess _____
4. Hunt's _____

5. Hills Bros. _____
6. Campbell's _____
7. Wonder _____
8. Hershey's _____
9. Uncle Ben's _____
10. Aunt Jemima's _____
11. Velveeta _____
12. Wrigley's _____
13. Farmer John _____
14. Best Foods _____
15. Minute Maid _____

Q28. Fill in the blanks with foods:

1. She was a beautiful _____ blonde.
2. Life's no bowl of _____.
3. Not for all the _____ in China!
4. The _____ doesn't fall very far from the tree.
5. Who's going to bring home the _____?
6. It's the greatest thing since sliced _____.
7. Yes, we have no _____.
8. He got caught with his hand in the _____ jar.
9. She dropped me like a hot _____.
10. I've got other _____ to fry.
11. That's the icing on the _____.
12. Last one there is a rotten _____.

Answers

Q24. 1. saltwater taffy   2. black licorice   3. candy canes
4. bubble gum   5. gum drops   6. cotton candy
7. cracker jacks   8. jelly beans   9. jaw breakers
10. caramel corn   11. peanut brittle   12. butterscotch toffee

Q25. 1. milk   2. goose   3. pudding   4. beans   5. soup   6. cake
7. egg   8. apple   9. cream   10. peas   11. nut   12. cracker
13. sandwich   14. grapes   15. pie   16. bananas   17. tea
18. peanuts   19. cookie   20. potato

Q26. 1. d   2. h   3. j   4. f   5. a   6. c   7. i   8. b   9. g   10. e   11. d
12. f   13. g   14. h   15. i   16. j   17. b   18. c   19. a   20. e

Q27. 1. root beer   2. baby food   3. cupcakes
4. catsup   5. coffee   6. soup   7. bread
8. chocolate   9. rice   10. pancakes
11. cheese   12. gum   13. meats
14. mayonnaise   15. juices

Q28. 1. strawberry   2. cherries   3. tea
4. apple   5. bacon   6. bread
7. bananas   8. cookie   9. potato
10. fish   11. cake   12. egg

**Give yourself 1 point for every
correct answer:** _____

Got their hands in
the cookie jar

A LITTLE HISTORY

- The expression **eating humble pie** comes from a time in Old
  England when servants were fed leftover animal parts, such as deer
  entrails, in baked pies. So they ate the ***umble pie***, while the choice
  cuts were being served to their masters nearby.
- Organ grinders and their dancing monkeys were a common site in
  American cities during the late 1800s. After the monkey performed,
  it was often rewarded with a banana. **Going bananas** still refers to
  wild and crazy behavior today.

BORN IN THE U.S.A.

- America is a land of immigrants. This is just a taste of their
  influence:

beef Stroganoff	**(Russian)**
pizza, ravioli, and lasagna	**(Italian)**
shish kabobs	**(Middle Eastern)**
bratwurst and sauerkraut	**(German)**
stir fry with white rice	**(Chinese)**

SAY IT RIGHT

- Not everyone uses the same word to name things:

  lollypop = sucker
  sub = grinder
  flapjacks = pancakes
  yams = sweet potatoes
  cantaloupe = melon
  sweet rolls = Danish

ON YOUR OWN

1. *Have ever been to a **smorgasbord**?*
2. *Which do you like more—**popsicles** or **snow cones**?*
3. *Have you ever eaten at a **greasy spoon**?*
4. *Do you enjoy **cakewalking** or **apple bobbing**?*
5. *Have you ever tried **chitlins**?*

WORDS OF WISDOM

"A hot dog at the ball park is better than steak at the Ritz."

Humphrey Bogart

V. ANIMAL LOVER!

Q29. Try some words and expressions that refer to the animal
kingdom. Do you know which ones go together best?

1. ugly		a. dog	
2. leap		b. shark	
3. red		c. worm	
4. eager		d. horse	
5. stool		e. steer	
6. road		f. elephant	
7. card		g. puppy	
8. love		h. bird	
9. book		i. sheep	
10. bum		j. beaver	
11. hot		k. herring	
12. white		l. duckling	
13. black		m. pigeon	
14. hush		n. frog	
15. dark		o. hog	

Q30. Each one of these is missing the name of an animal:

1. Charlie _____
2. Mickey _____
3. Jack _____
4. Porky _____
5. Bugs _____
6. Billy _____
7. Teddy _____
8. Bob _____
9. Jiminy _____
10. Daffy _____

Q31. These next expressions need animals to get them started. But first, you'll need to unscramble the letters here to form a list:

XOF	_____	LEEGA	_____	ROHES	_____
NHKICE	_____	TRA	_____	BIRTAB	_____
NOYKME	_____	GOH	_____	WASN	_____
IGP	_____	PPU	_____	GOD	_____

1. I'm tired of this _____ race.
2. My cousin is an _____ scout.
3. Did you see his _____ tags?
4. We danced the _____ trot.
5. I had to wear my _____ suit.
6. He hit me with a _____ punch.
7. They slept in a _____ tent.
8. This job pays _____ feed.
9. The kids were speaking _____ Latin.
10. This is her last game, her _____ song.
11. Everyone went _____ wild at the party.
12. I've got my lucky _____ shoe.

Q32. More creatures are required here:

1. Something's wrong; I smell a _____.	a. donkey
2. You really took the _____ by the horns.	b. monkey
3. Do that again, and you're a dead _____.	c. horse
4. _____ got your tongue?	d. rat
5. I think that stuff is for the _____.	e. goose
6. She'll make a _____ out of him.	f. bull
7. Let's not open another can of _____.	g. birds
8. We're on another wild _____ chase.	h. duck
9. Pin the tail on the _____!	i. worms
10. Get off your high _____.	j. cat

Keep going!

11. That's a _____ of another color.   a. alligator
12. Don't play cat and _____ with me!   b. fish
13. She let the _____ out of the bag.   c. hog
14. You can complain until the _____ come home. d. mouse
15. We're sitting _____ if we stay here.   e. dog
16. He ran like a _____ out of hell.   f. horse
17. See you later, _____.   g. ducks
18. They were living high off the _____.   h. cat
19. Every _____ has its day.   i. cows
20. I felt like a _____ out of water.   j. bat

Answers

Q29. 1. l 2. n 3. k 4. j 5. m 6. o
　　7. b 8. h 9. c 10. e
　　11. a 12. f 13. i 14. g 15. d

Q30. 1. horse 2. mouse 3. rabbit
　　4. pig 5. bunny 6. goat
　　7. bear 8. cat 9. cricket
　　10. duck

Q31. 1. rat 2. eagle 3. dog
　　4. fox 5. monkey 6. rabbit
　　7. pup 8. chicken 9. pig
　　10. swan 11. hog 12. horse

Q32. 1. d 2. f 3. h 4. j 5. g 6. b
　　7. i 8. e 9. a 10. c 11. f
　　12. d 13. h 14. i 15. g
　　16. j 17. a 18. c
　　19. e 20. b

Brainwashing

___

__Give yourself 1 point for every correct answer:__ _____

ALL-AMERICAN CROSSWORD 1

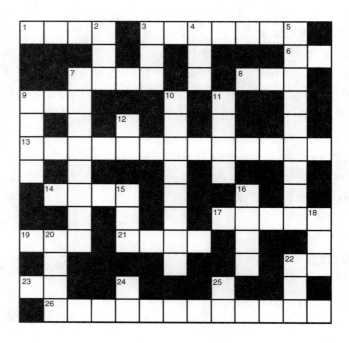

Across

1. _____ will be the day!
3. I'm _____ as punch.
6. We're _____ the money… .
7. It's thick as pea _____.
8. Step on the _____!
9. I smell a ____.
13. (Means lazy or dawdling)
14. I don't have a _____.
17. The chairman of the _____.
19. The hobo traveled in a box ____.
21. _____ around the rosey… .
22. ___ that as it may.
23. Boy ___ boy!
26. (Means secret listener)

Down

  2. No _____ ways about it.
  3. ____! Goes the weasel.
  4. I've got my _____ on you.
  5. He's as dull as _____.
  7. She's a _____ for details.
  9. He likes to _____ the roost.
 10. You're _____ my style.
 11. The die is _____.
 12. C'est ___ vie.
 15. She gave him an ___ful.
 16. That's just a _____ and bull story.
 18. (Means female deer)
 20. I've got a belly_____.
 22. He's busy as a ____.
 24. ___, myself, and I.
 25. ___ way, José.

A finished crossword is on page 241.

BORN IN THE U.S.A.

- Based on size, age, or breeding, Americans will call their dog a **pooch**, a **hound**, a **pup**, a **mutt**, or a **mongrel**. But most will agree that the dog is still man's best friend:

  > In this **dog-eat-dog world** that's **gone to the dogs, every dog has its day**.

- Americans say **watch the birdie** at photo time, put their money in a **piggy bank**, carry their leftovers in a **doggie bag**, and claim that a **stork delivered the baby**. In finance, the market is either **bearish** or **bullish**, while in Washington **hawks** and **doves** battle for their political parties, which are represented by **donkeys** and **elephants**!

SAY IT RIGHT

- Some names of animals in America are actually compound words. Notice the descriptions:

blood hound	**hoot owl**	**rattle snake**
prairie dog	**lady bug**	**blow fish**
sea horse	**fire fly**	**bald eagle**
alley cat	**ground hog**	**mountain lion**

Certain breeds or species are common, too:

*He owned four **palominos**, two **heifers**, one **Dalmatian**, and six **Siamese**.*

A LITTLE HISTORY

- **Living high off the hog**, an old Southern expression, suggests that eating pork chops and ribs (the upper parts of a pig) is better than eating some of the less appealing *lower parts*.
- During the Middle Ages, cheating merchants would put cat meat into their customers' bags instead of providing them with the pork or beef they had ordered. Nothing would be suspected until they returned home and **let the cat out of the bag**. Today, it simply means to give away a secret.
- Physicians once believed that the secretions of a frog could cure any throat ailment, so they often put the amphibians in their patients' mouths until they felt the treatment was complete. Today, **having a frog in your throat** loses the original meaning and only indicates that you are not able to speak loudly or clearly.

ON YOUR OWN

1. *Do you know anyone who is **pigheaded**?*
2. *Use the words **bullpen** and **guppy** in the same sentence.*
3. *Do you own a **rubber ducky** or know a **fish story**?*
4. *Do you know the tune to **"How Much Is that Doggie in the Window"**?*

Talk turkey

Q33. Take the two words, and come up with a classic comment that
refers to critters:

1. snug/ rug   <u>**I was as snug as a bug in a rug.**</u>
2. plenty/ sea   _____
3. straight/ mouth   _____
4. cat/ play   _____
5. hand/ bush   _____
6. cats/ dogs   _____
7. early/ worm   _____
8. pearls/ swine   _____
9. wrench/ machinery _____
10. wolf/ clothing   _____
11. bull/ closet   _____
12. good/ gander   _____
13. feather/ flock   _____
14. teach/ tricks   _____
15. count/ hatch   _____

Q34. Choose now the best beast to finish these phrases:

1. She spent her night counting _____.   a. turkey
2. You're making a mountain out of a _____hill.   b. horse
3. That boy likes to _____ his sisters.   c. hog
4. He used to cry _____.   d. crow
5. They _____ tied him.   e. worm
6. Let's talk _____.   f. mole
7. He likes to _____ around.   g. goat
8. I'll make you eat _____.   h. bug
9. You can't _____ your way out of this one.   i. wolf
10. That really gets my _____.   j. sheep

Q35. **What** animals are they talking about?

1. Let sleeping **what** lie?   a. _____
2. **What** other tail can you wear besides pigtails?   b. _____
3. I ran around like a **what** with its head cut off?   c. _____
4. **What** do you have in your pants?   d. _____
5. You hit the eye of a **what** in the dart game?   e. _____
6. It's five miles as the **what** flies?   f. _____
7. A little **what** told you?   g. _____
8. The straw broke the back of a **what**?   h. _____
9. You're pulling a **what** out of a hat?   i. _____
10. She was crying **what** kind of tears?   j. _____

Q36. Insert animals only, please.

1. I rubbed my lucky _____'s foot.
2. It was a _____ of a game.
3. I think the teacher wants to use me as a guinea _____.
4. It's like water off a _____'s back.
5. You can lead a _____ to water, but you can't make it drink.
6. There's more than one way to skin a _____.
7. We were sitting around shooting the _____.
8. I lost at the table when I rolled _____ eyes.
9. That movie gave me _____ bumps.
10. He just lay there playing _____.

Answers

Q33. 2. There are plenty of fish in the sea.

3. I heard it straight from the horse's mouth.

4. While the cat's away, the mice will play.

5. A bird in the hand is worth two in the bush.

6. It's raining cats and dogs.

7. The early bird catches the worm.

8. Don't cast your pearls before swine.

9. That threw the monkey wrench into the machinery.

10. He's a wolf in sheep's clothing.

11. You're like a bull in a china closet.

12. What is good for the goose is good for the gander.

13. Birds of a feather flock together.

14. You can't teach an old dog new tricks.

15. Don't count your chickens before they hatch.

Q34. 1. j 2. f 3. h 4. i 5. c 6. a 7. b 8. d 9. e 10. g

Q35. 1. dogs 2. pony 3. chicken 4. ants 5. bull's 6. crow
7. bird 8. camel 9. rabbit 10. crocodile

Q36. 1. rabbit 2. whale 3. pig 4. duck 5. horse 6. cat 7. bull
8. snake 9. goose 10. possum

Behind the eight-ball

Give yourself 1 point for every correct answer:

A LITTLE HISTORY

Some expressions are ancient and come from distant places, but Americans have used them so often that they are now part of our cultural landscape.

- **Casting pearls before swine** comes from the Bible (Matthew 7:6). It refers to wasting something valuable on a person who doesn't appreciate it. Some people are unable to appreciate higher levels of being and prefer to live in ignorance (like animals), and to help them would be a waste of our time.

- **Crying wolf** comes from one of Aesop's fables, where a shepherd boy falsely cried out that a wolf was attacking his sheep. After a while, people began to ignore him, so when a real wolf finally did attack, the boy's cries went unnoticed. Today, the expression still implies sending out a false alarm of danger.

- **A bird in the hand is worth two in the bush** means that something guaranteed is worth a lot more than just a promise. This ancient Greek saying referred to bird hunters who claimed that having one guaranteed meal in hand was better than waiting around for the big catch.

WORDS OF WISDOM

"A chicken doesn't stop scratching just because worms are scarce."

Anonymous

WHAT'S MY SCORE?

TOTAL CORRECT: _____

TOTAL POSSIBLE: ___449___

Chapter Two

Special Detail

VI. ALL KINDS OF STUFF!

Q1. What typical idioms these are! And all you need is to add things that are missing.

1. They're eating me out of _____ and home.	a.	wind
2. The _____ is falling! The _____ is falling!	b.	stick
3. It looks like we're all in the same _____.	c.	towel
4. You're barking up the wrong _____.	d.	handle
5. Knock on _____.	e.	bell
6. I don't mean to burst your _____.	f.	bush
7. Don't fly off the _____.	g.	guns
8. That's no _____ of roses.	h.	boat
9. Stop beating around the _____.	i.	bed
10. We were saved by the _____.	j.	wall
11. The _____ have turned.	k.	tacks
12. The handwriting is on the _____.	l.	strings
13. He's getting the short end of the _____.	m.	town
14. Let's get down to brass _____.	n.	house
15. You couldn't hold a _____ to her.	o.	candle
16. Stick to your _____.	p.	wood
17. I'll have to pull some _____.	q.	sky
18. Why not throw caution to the _____.	r.	tables
19. She's the toast of the _____.	s.	tree
20. Tell him to throw in the _____.	t.	bubble

Q2. Sometimes the same word works for two expressions:

1. Who wears the _____ in your family? They scared the _____ off of me!	a.	sleeve
	b.	hat
2. If the _____ fits, wear it. The _____ is on the other foot.	c.	collar
	d.	belt
3. He'd give the _____ off his back. Keep your _____ on!	e.	shirt
	f.	boots
4. You bet your _____!	g.	glove
5. That's another feather in his _____.	h.	shoe

6. At the drop of a _____.   i. cap
7. She's a little hot under the _____.   j. pants
8. Nothing up my _____!
9. It fits like a _____.
10. He's going to have to tighten his _____.

Q3. Try using these words to form every day phrases about THINGS:

1. **Rock** the **boat**
2. _____ the _____   ROCK   BITE   FORT   MUSTARD
3. _____ the _____   GUN   BREAK   BOAT   FACE
4. _____ the _____   BULLET   HIT   HATCHET   KICK
5. _____ the _____   HOLD   MUSIC   CUT   JUMP
6. _____ the _____   ICE   BURY   SACK   BUCKET
7. _____ the _____
8. _____ the _____
9. _____ the _____
10. _____ the _____

Answers

Q1. 1. n   2. q   3. h   4. s   5. p
6. t   7. d   8. i   9. f   10. e
11. r   12. j   13. b   14. k
15. o   16. g   17. l   18. a
19. m   20. c

Q2. 1. j   2. h   3. e   4. f   5. i
6. b   7. c   8. a   9. g   10. d

Q3. (Any order.) bite the bullet,
hold the fort, cut the mustard,
jump the gun, break the ice,
face the music, kick the bucket,
hit the sack, bury the hatchet

Like finding a needle
in a haystack

Give yourself 1 point for every correct answer: _____

BORN IN THE U.S.A.

- The hat and cap are around with many Americans today. Check out these other expressions that mention head coverings:

  *It's a secret, so **hide it under your hat**.*
  *They **passed the hat** and took a collection.*
  *I need **to take off my hat to you**, and offer my congratulations.*

- And how many words we have to name the same thing! Especially if it is unpleasant.

  I got fired, canned, shafted. They gave me the axe, the boot, the pink slip, the heave-ho, and my walking papers!!

SAY IT RIGHT

- These words mean the same thing depending on where you live.

icebox— fridge	**comics—funnies**
davenport—couch	**recliner—easy chair**
family room—den	**soft drink—soda pop**

A LITTLE HISTORY

- For years, informal races of various types were signaled to start when a person at the finish line would **drop his hat**. Today, any impulsive act is said to be done **at the drop of a hat**.
- Raccoon hunting was a popular sport during colonial times, and it was not uncommon for one's dogs to occasionally **bark up the wrong tree** sometime during the chase. It's now used to mean that you're on the incorrect path during a pursuit.
- When criminals were hanged in early America, in some cases they had to stand on a bucket with a noose around their neck. The hanging was complete after the hangman **kicked the bucket** from under the victims' legs. Now it is simply another way of saying that a person died.

Q4. These are always fun. Create a common expression using the two words provided:

1. cloud/ lining
2. needle/ haystack
3. chips/ may
4. home/ castle
5. book/ cover
6. bark/ bite
7. variety/ life
8. spoon/ mouth
9. money/ trees
10. glass/ stones

Stars in your eyes

Q5. What thing is missing in these sentences?

1. the got tail by I've the   _____
2. that's bounces way the the   _____
3. the you head the hit   _____
4. irons the you've too in many got   _____
5. out you're the yet of not   _____

Q6. Any last words?

1. Champing at the _____   a. stone
2. Flash in the _____   b. city
3. Doesn't ring a _____   c. bit
4. Afraid of his own _____   d. horn
5. All set in _____   e. stitches
6. Toot my own _____   f. bell
7. Need to change your _____   g. thoughts
8. She had me in _____   h. pan
9. Penny for your _____   i. shadow
10. The key to the _____   j. tune

Q7. Now put these things together to form new words or phrases:

1.	snow	a.	drive
2.	hay	b.	wagon
3.	paper	c.	shot
4.	memory	d.	check
5.	band	e.	job
6.	wishing	f.	page
7.	rain	g.	lane
8.	flag	h.	well
9.	snap	i.	salute
10.	front	j.	wire

Answers

Q4. 1. Every cloud has a silver lining.
2. It's like finding a needle in a haystack.
3. Let the chips fall where they may.
4. A man's home is his castle.
5. You can't judge a book by its cover.
6. His bark is worse than his bite.
7. Variety is the spice of life.
8. He was born with a silver spoon in his mouth.
9. Money doesn't grow on trees.
10. People who live in glass houses should not throw stones.

Q5. 1. world   2. ball   3. nail   4. fire   5. woods
Q6. 1. c   2. h   3. f   4. i   5. a   6. d   7. j   8. e   9. g   10. b
Q7. 1. e   2. j   3. a   4. g   5. b   6. h   7. d   8. i   9. c   10. f

Give yourself 1 point for every correct answer:

A LITTLE HISTORY

- In the upper crust of American society, it was once customary to offer a silver spoon as a gift to a newborn baby. As a result, anyone today who is born of wealth and privilege is considered **born with a silver spoon in his mouth**.
- When you pulled the trigger on an old musket, sparks ignited the gunpowder in a small pan and caused the weapon to fire. Sometimes it didn't, which is why anyone who doesn't live up to his or her potential today is called a **flash in the pan**.

BORN IN THE U.S.A.

- As you can guess, references to money in America are everywhere:

    *It only costs one thin **dime**, but it isn't worth a **plug nickel**. Saving your bucks for the nest egg? **Penny-wise** and **pound foolish!***
    *Old **moneybags' pocket** was burning, so he dropped a grand at the track.*

ON YOUR OWN

1. *Have you ever been **shaking in your boots**?*
2. *Name someone who is **too big for his britches**.*
3. *Who would you buy **booties** for?*
4. *Who's still tied to his **mother's apron strings**?*

WORDS OF WISDOM

"Nothing is certain but death and taxes."

Benjamin Franklin

VII. BITS AND PIECES!

Big frog in a small pond

Q8. There are still a few more things ahead. Fill in the missing words in both columns, and then join the ones that match:

1. We've come full **circle (i)**
2. My back's to the _____
3. I'm at my wit's _____
4. He's got a one-_____ mind
5. Stand your _____!
6. That really hit the _____
7. Make yourself at _____
8. Let's play a _____ on her
9. Mum's the _____!
10. It's the _____ of gravity
11. He's a thorn in my _____
12. A new lease on _____
13. She popped the _____
14. It's food for _____
15. She had _____ in her eyes

a. You're on the right _____
b. I lost my train of _____
c. It's out of the _____
d. I cracked a _____
e. Count your lucky _____
f. She went off the deep _____
g. You were the _____ of the party
h. He took the _____ in his own hands
i. It's a vicious _____
j. To be on the safe _____
k. This _____ has ears
l. Keep the _____ fires burning
m. By _____ of mouth
n. I've got a soft _____ for her
o. We've covered a lot of _____

Q9. Do you think you know American? Try these!

1. Your _____ is as good as mine.
2. I've got an _____ to grind.
3. I had the _____ of my life.
4. Don't press your _____.
5. You missed by a _____.
6. It's all in a day's _____.
7. He pulled the _____ right out from under me.
8. Don't upset the apple _____.
9. Get to the _____ .
10. She turned over a new _____.

a. cart
b. leaf
c. point
d. rug
e. work
f. time
g. guess
h. luck
i. mile
j. ax

Answers

Q8. 2. wall (k)   3. end (f)   4. track (a)   5. ground (o)   6. spot (n)
  7. home (l)   8. joke (d)   9. word (m)   10. law (h)   11. side (j)
  12. life (g)   13. question (c)   14. thought (b)   15. stars (e)
Q9. 1. g   2. j   3. f   4. h   5. i   6. e   7. d   8. a   9. c   10. b

Give yourself 1 point for every correct answer: _____

BORN IN THE U.S.A.

• Look at the variations of *another* and *other* among these:

> *Don't give it **another** thought. You see, one thing always leads to **another**, so soon you'll be dancing to **another** tune.*
> *Who looked the **other** way when I smiled? It was none **other** than Nancy. Oh well, I'll just turn the **other** cheek. There are plenty of **other** fish in the sea.*

A LITTLE HISTORY

- **Turning over a new leaf** dates back to the 1600s, and refers to turning the page in one's diary. Since the next day brought new opportunities for improvement, the expression began to imply reform or chances of a fresh start.
- **To upset the applecart** means to interfere with another's plan or program. Dating back to the Romans, the phrase depicts a messy scene in busy traffic, when one person creates a major disturbance by causing a fruit merchant's cart to spill onto the street.

WORDS OF WISDOM

"If you want to know the value of money, try to borrow some."

Benjamin Franklin

Q10. These have answers, too, but you'll need to unscramble some letters first:

1. He's turning over in his _____	a. UGN
2. They lived off the fat of the _____	b. OSHUE
3. Reach for the _____!	c. LRADOL
4. You drive a hard _____	d. SWAH
5. I drew a total _____	e. AERVG
6. Drinks are on the _____	f. DALN
7. He's full of hot _____	g. KYS
8. It all comes out in the _____	h. RIA
9. You can bet your bottom _____	i. LAKNB
10. He's one crazy son of a _____	j. INAARBG

Q11. Here everything's in the plural:

1. He pulled out all the _____	a. nickels
2. No _____ attached	b. coals
3. Don't take any wooden _____	c. colors
4. Please don't mince _____	d. tricks
5. It'll be _____ for you	e. cleaners

6. She raked me over the _____   f. strings

7. He took me to the _____   g. dollars

8. We passed with flying _____   h. words

9. I'll need my bag of _____   i. stops

10. I feel like a million _____   j. curtains

Q12. Did you know that **hooey**, **bunk**, **hokum**, **twaddle**, **humbug**, **hogwash**, and **clap-trap** all mean the same thing? Take these other popular words and match them to their meanings:

CHEAP

White elephant sale

1. a trim   a. a contraption

2. a hunch   b. a joke

3. a gag   c. a black eye

4. a flop   d. a pushover

5. a shiner   e. a stroke of luck

6. a lift   f. a hole in the wall

7. a fluke   g. a gut feeling

8. a cinch   h. a ride

9. a gizmo   i. a fiasco

10. a dive   j. a haircut

Q13. All of the following words can be used to create well-known expressions.

1. frying pan/fire   **I jumped from the frying pan right into the fire.**

2. light/tunnel   _____

3. side/bed   _____

4. chip/block   _____

5. wind/sails   _____

6. penny/earned   _____

7. blood/water   _____

8. actions/words   _____

9. honesty/policy   _____

10. candle/ends   _____

Answers

Q10. 1. e   2. f   3. g   4. j   5. i   6. b   7. h   8. d   9. c   10. a

Q11. 1. i   2. f   3. a   4. h   5. j   6. b   7. e   8. c   9. d   10. g

Q12. 1. j   2. g   3. b   4. i   5. c   6. h   7. e   8. d   9. a   10. f

Q13. (Answers may vary.)

    2. I see the light at the end of the tunnel.

    3. I got up on the wrong side of the bed.

    4. He's a chip off the old block.

    5. It took the wind out of my sails.

    6. A penny saved is a penny earned.

    7. Blood is thicker than water.

    8. Actions speak louder than words.

    9. Honesty is the best policy.

   10. You can't burn the candle at both ends.

Give yourself 1 point for every correct answer:

A LITTLE HISTORY

- In the seventeenth century, anyone who had to work from early morning to late at night literally had to burn candles at **both ends of the day** in order to have light. Over time, the expression for tireless activity was shortened to simply, **burning the candle at both ends**.

- In the 1800s, a lottery ticket that didn't win was called a **blank**. When a person drew a blank, they felt disappointment. Today, **drawing a blank** refers to failing as well, but only as it relates to remembering something.

ON YOUR OWN

1. *Have you ever fallen for something **hook, line, and sinker**?*
2. *Have you ever bought anything **lock, stock, and barrel**?*

BORN IN THE U.S.A.

- What in the **world** is happening here?

*John is **out of this world**; he's **setting the world on fire** and really **moving up in the world**. I think the world of him, even though he **lives in a world of his own**!*

VIII. TELL ME ABOUT IT!

Q14. What descriptive words are missing here?

1. She's skating on _____ ice.	a. blue
2. It's brand _____.	b. bad
3. He's a _____ -blooded killer.	c. long
4. Home _____ home.	d. hot
5. It's too _____ to handle.	e. back
6. To make a _____ story short.	f. sweet
7. It's up in the wild _____ yonder.	g. flat
8. Let's put it on the _____ burner.	h. thin
9. _____ news travels fast.	i. cold
10. I'm _____ broke.	j. new

Q15. Try to link two words together!

1. dead	a. meal
2. cold	b. moon
3. last	c. shave
4. square	d. shot
5. long	e. crack
6. close	f. straw
7. small	g. cream
8. full	h. face
9. wise	i. heat
10. happy	j. world

Cast pearls before swine

Q16. Americans use all kinds of colors to describe. Which go together best?

1. red	a. elephant
2. silver	b. thumb
3. blue	c. market
4. green	d. area
5. gold	e. carpet
6. yellow	f. juice
7. white	g. moon
8. black	h. lining
9. gray	i. rush
10. orange	j. belly

Answers

Q14. 1. h   2. j   3. i   4. f   5. d   6. c   7. a   8. e   9. b   10. g

Q15. 1. i   2. g   3. f   4. a   5. d   6. c   7. j   8. b   9. e   10. h

Q16. 1. e   2. h   3. g   4. b   5. i   6. j   7. a   8. c   9. d   10. f

Give yourself 1 point for every correct answer:

A LITTLE HISTORY

- In horse racing, a hotly contested race around the track is called a **heat**. For years, heats were simply counted until a horse won. Sometimes, however, the horses tied, so the heat was considered **dead** or nullified. Today, **dead heat** refers to any tight race or tie.
- In India, having a white elephant is considered sacred, so owning one meant that your beast of burden could never work. Being a very practical people, for us a **white elephant** is any unwanted household item that is given away.
- Science once believed that there was a relationship between human emotions and the temperature of one's blood; therefore, a **cold-blooded** person lacked emotion, and was capable of hurting others without feeling anything. Being **hot-blooded** wasn't good either, because it would lead to explosive outbursts. Evidently, normal people were somewhere in-between.

ON YOUR OWN

1. *Do you have a **clean bill of health** or must you wear a **straight jacket** sometimes?*
2. *Do you know anyone who is **flaky? Savvy?***
3. *You haven't the **foggiest** what?*
4. *Name someone who wears a **hard hat**.*

SAY IT RIGHT

- Ah, pronunciation. Notice how many descriptive words end with the letters "ed," but are pronounced differently:

    The disturbed man in the padded cell told a barefaced lie.

- Some classic expressions include two descriptive words:

    My spoiled rotten cousin lived to the ripe old age of 100!

WORDS OF WISDOM

"True happiness is not attained through self-gratification, but through fidelity to a worthy cause."

Helen Keller

Q17. These words are a bit tricky. Find the definitions:

1. lousy	a. silly
2. fishy	b. moody
3. corny	c. creepy
4. jumpy	d. nifty
5. touchy	e. groggy
6. spiffy	f. crummy
7. nippy	g. crabby
8. woozy	h. shifty
9. spooky	i. chilly
10. ornery	j. edgy

Q18. Unscramble these words to create five two-word expressions:

1. <u>SPITTING IMAGE</u>   HEART   STOCK   STANDING
2. _____   THINKING   LAUGHING   IMAGE
3. _____   OVATION   CAP   BLEEDING
4. _____   SPITTING
5. _____

Q19. With the following, only the first letter of a descriptive word is provided:

1. It's survival of the **f**_____.
2. It was off the **b** _____ track.
3. I was scared **s** _____.
4. It's **d** _____ cheap.
5. She dropped him like a **h** _____ potato.
6. It's burnt to a **c** _____.
7. I'm tickled **p** _____.
8. They're **t** _____ than nails.
9. The bill was paid in **f** _____.
10. Practice makes **p** _____.
11. I love **d** _____ **h** _____ cooking.
12. He asked her out of the **c** _____ **b** _____ sky.
13. She wore a **p** _____ **d** _____ bikini.
14. I got stuck in **n** _____ **m** _____'s land.
15. He went through it with a **f** _____ **t** _____ comb.

Answers
Q17. 1. f 2. h 3. a 4. j 5. b 6. d 7. i 8. e 9. c 10. g
Q18. (Any order.)
    2. bleeding heart   3. laughing stock   4. standing ovation
    5. thinking cap
Q19. 1. fittest   2. beaten   3. stiff   4. dirt   5. hot   6. crisp
    7. pink   8. tougher   9. full   10. perfect   11. down home
    12. clear blue   13. polka dot   14. no man   15. fine tooth

Give yourself 1 point for every correct answer:

BORN IN THE U.S.A.

- American English is full of **nothings**:

  She's nothing to look at—nothing but skin and bones, but *she can do the job in nothing flat. It's nothing short of a miracle!*

- American English can be pretty descriptive:

  I used to be a bug-eyed, buck-toothed, snot-nosed runt. I lived with my bleached-blonde aunt, who was usually plastered and all tuckered out. It was pretty glum. She was just a lonely, washed-up showgirl with bags under her eyes and a swelled head.

A LITTLE HISTORY

- Centuries ago, the expression **spit and image** made reference to any two people who had such a close resemblance that even their saliva was alike. It is believed that **spitting image** evolved from that expression.
- Most American pioneers had to dig wells to have consistent access to water. During the process, they often ended up with large piles of extra dirt, which was a real pain to move. As a result, dirt was free to anyone willing to haul it away. Consequently, anything that is **dirt cheap** today is extremely inexpensive.
- British Admiral Edward Vernon, nicknamed **Old Grog** because of the grogram cloak he always wore, introduced the Navy custom of serving rum mixed with water. The drink became known as **grog**, and anyone found stumbling around the dock was called **groggy**. Today, the word refers to a feeling of sluggishness or weakness in the legs.

Step on one's toes

ON YOUR OWN

1. *Define or use each of these in a sentence:*

   Big Foot   **Scot-free**   **Scout's Honor**

2. *Explain a **close call**, a **cold call**, and a **last call**.*
3. *Have you ever met a **one-of-a-kind**, **happy-go-lucky good-for-nothing**?*

WORDS OF WISDOM

"It's a recession when your neighbor loses his job; it's a depression when you lose yours."

Harry S. Truman

Q20. In the following activity, the same descriptive word fits into both sentences:

1. We hunted _____ and low. She left me _____ and dry.
2. Let's get something _____. I couldn't keep a _____ face.
3. We paid our _____ respects. That's the _____ straw.
4. I feel like a _____ person. I turned over a _____ leaf.
5. Remember the good _____ days. That's _____ hat.
6. Get this through your _____ skull. He's pouring it on _____.
7. It serves you _____. Step _____ up.
8. It appeared out of _____ air. I'm spreading myself out too _____.
9. Are we on the _____ page? By the _____ token.
10. Don't sell yourself _____. I got the _____ end of the stick.
11. It's too good to be _____. It's a dream come _____.
12. On _____ thought, I'll go. I've got my _____ wind.
13. You're digging your _____ grave. I can hold my _____.
14. He was out _____. I broke out in a _____ sweat.
15. It's too _____ to be true. Your guess is as _____ as mine.

Q21. Here, comparisons are made with the word **like**. Fix the words
in the second column and then start:

1.	He took off like a _____ out of hell.	a.	GLTHI
2.	She's got a memory like an _____.	b.	GRUESALTH
3.	It's like taking candy from a _____.	c.	CKOTAESH
4.	We were like two peas in a _____.	d.	LESET
5.	He was out like a _____.	e.	ZCAYR
6.	You lie like a _____.	f.	OKBO
7.	She sat there like a _____ on a log.	g.	DOP
8.	I felt like a _____ out of water.	h.	AGGN
9.	They were led like lambs to the _____.	i.	GRU
10.	It was like _____ off a duck's back.	j.	GODS
11.	It went like clock_____.	k.	TEREH
12.	It's like walking on _____.	l.	MPBU
13.	You look like the _____.	m.	REWAT
14.	We fought like cats and _____.	n.	ETTEH
15.	It was like a _____-ring circus.	o.	HISF
16.	It was like pulling _____.	p.	VILED
17.	They were selling like _____.	q.	LNMOIIL
18.	They came on like _____busters.	r.	KROW
19.	Like father, like _____.	s.	LAPEENTH
20.	She ran like a chicken with its _____ cut off.	t.	RMOWORTO
21.	I feel like a _____ dollars.	u.	LGESEGLH
22.	He has a mind like a _____ trap.	v.	YABB
23.	I can read you like a _____.	w.	ABT
24.	We worked like _____.	x.	EHAD
25.	They were working like there's no _____.	y.	NSO

Q22. Make the best connection as you form more common phrases:

1.	clean	a.	street
2.	evil	b.	stand
3.	close	c.	tale
4.	free	d.	robin
5.	easy	e.	shake
6.	round	f.	shot
7.	tall	g.	eye
8.	long	h.	knit
9.	grand	i.	reign
10.	fair	j.	slate

Q23. These descriptions deal with the animal kingdom:

1. fat	a. goose
2. dumb	b. fox
3. silly	c. steer
4. clumsy	d. butterfly
5. lone	e. cat
6. eager	f. duck
7. sly	g. wolf
8. social	h. beaver
9. lame	i. ox
10. bum	j. bunny

Answers

Q20. 1. high 2. straight 3. last 4. new 5. old 6. thick
7. right 8. thin 9. same 10. short 11. true 12. second
13. own 14. cold 15. good

Q21. 1. w 2. s 3. v 4. g 5. a 6. i 7. l 8. o 9. b 10. m
11. r 12. u 13. p 14. j 15. k 16. n 17. c 18. h 19. y
20. x 21. q 22. d 23. f 24. e 25. t

Q22. 1. j 2. g 3. h 4. i 5. a 6. d 7. c 8. f 9. b 10. e

Q23. 1. e 2. j 3. a 4. i 5. g 6. h 7. b 8. d 9. f 10. c

Give yourself 1 point for every correct answer:

Don't look a gift
horse in the mouth

A LITTLE HISTORY

- During the Revolutionary Period, a traveler's dinner plate consisted of a square piece of wood with a bowl carved out in the middle. When a person stopped at either a home or an inn, he or she was served from the kettle that was cooking over the fire. The ideal situation was to acquire three **square meals** a day.
- In the 1800s, long before hot dogs and cotton candy, local fairs boasted of having the best hotcakes around, which eventually became a popular breakfast food across the country. As a result, the expression **selling like hotcakes** became the cry whenever a new product sold well and was flying off the shelves.
- Surprisingly, the phrase, **fair shake** has nothing to do with the shaking of hands. The **shake** comes from the game of dice, where trustworthy gentlemen would toss the dice from cups without any trickery or deceit.

BORN IN THE U.S.A.

- Americans tend to be individualistic, taking pride in doing things all by themselves. Note how often people will say they did it on their own:

> *I mind **my own** business, stand on **my own** two feet, don't know **my own** strength, dig **my own** grave, cut **my own** throat, take the law into **my own** hands, blow **my own** horn, and take a dose of **my own** medicine!*

ON YOUR OWN

1. *Have you ever **screamed like a banshee?***
2. *Have you ever **looked like the cat that swallowed the canary?***
3. *Have you ever come out of it **smelling like a rose?***

SAY IT RIGHT

- When comparing people to animals, the key is to be as graphic as possible:

    She eats like a bird.
    She eats like a horse.
    She eats like a pig.

- And there are no rules when it comes to making comparisons:

    He worked like crazy.
    He worked like nobody's business.
    He worked like the blazes.

Q24. These expressions may or may not have an exact answer, but the meaning should be one and one only. Give them a try.

1. Big as a _____
2. Black as _____
3. Good as _____
4. Thick as _____
5. Weak as a _____
6. Cold as _____
7. Dead as a _____
8. Dry as a _____
9. Easy as _____
10. Fit as a _____
11. Flat as a _____
12. Free as a _____
13. Happy as a _____
14. Hard as _____
15. High as a _____
16. Hot as a _____
17. Soft as a _____
18. Light as a _____
19. Mad as a _____
20. Smart as a _____
21. Old as the _____
22. Clear as a _____

23. Poor as a _____
24. Pretty as a _____
25. Quick as a _____
26. Quiet as a _____
27. Right as _____
28. Sharp as a _____
29. Sly as a _____
30. Smooth as _____
31. Strong as an _____
32. Thin as a _____
33. Tough as _____
34. Ugly as _____
35. Cool as a _____

In one ear and out the other

Answers

Q24. 1. house, mountain   2. pitch, coal   3. gold   4. pea soup
     5. lamb   6. ice   7. dodo, doornail   8. bone
     9. apple pie, A-B-C, duck soup, sliced bread   10. fiddle
     11. pancake, board   12. bird   13. clam   14. stone, nails
     15. kite   16. pistol   17. baby's bottom   18. feather
     19. hatter, wet hen, hornet, March hare   20. whip   21. hills
     22. bell   23. church mouse   24. picture   25. wink, cat
     26. mouse   27. rain   28. tack   29. fox   30. silk   31. ox
     32. rail   33. nails   34. sin   35. cucumber

Give yourself 1 point for every correct answer: _____

A LITTLE HISTORY

- Originally, the expression **cool as a cucumber** referred to the preparation of cucumber salads, which were popular substitutes of hot dishes in the summer season. Later, the word **cool** took on another meaning, which was to remain calm under intense conflict or stress.
- Once upon a time in America, a homemade whistle carved out of wood was a common household toy. However, to get one to work, the whistle's air passage had to be cleared or cleaned regularly. Nowadays, **clean as a whistle** describes an excellent job of washing or tidying up.

SAY IT RIGHT

- Some people finish up their comparisons with generic phrases, such as **as all get out**, **as hell**, or **as can be**: It's as hot as all get out!
- Listen for clever compound expressions:

  It's as old as the hills and twice as dusty!

ON YOUR OWN

1. *Where would you find the **big hand**? The **big top**?*
2. *Have you ever experienced a **false alarm**? A **sock hop**? A **wild fling**?*
3. *When was the last time you had **easy pickings**?*

BORN IN THE U.S.A.

- Lots of folks talk BIG:

  *Today was my **big day** in the Big Apple. It was my **big moment** in sales. I was going to land the **big one**. But I didn't see the **big picture**. I opened my **big mouth** and told him I was **big-time**. He says, what's the **big idea**? You're just a **big frog** in a little pond! Oh, well, that's life in the **big city**! It's no **big deal**—I'm a **big girl**.*

WORDS OF WISDOM

"I think people want peace so much that one of these days governments had better get out of the way and let them have it."

Dwight D. Eisenhower

IX. TELL ME WHERE!

Q25. Expressions that refer to location? Fill in the blanks below:

1. We're working _____ the clock.	a. from
2. He screamed at the _____ of his voice.	b. out
3. She's really _____ to earth.	c. between
4. They've got me _____ a barrel.	d. behind
5. I have to get something _____ my chest.	e. under
6. He went _____ rags to riches.	f. back
7. You're reading _____ the lines.	g. within
8. I'm at the _____ of my rope.	h. through
9. She's _____ herself.	i. end
10. Let's keep it _____ wraps.	j. around
11. They put me _____ the ringer.	k. beside
12. Well, it's _____ to the drawing board.	l. down
13. She's a little _____ the times.	m. off
14. We're not _____ of the woods yet.	n. over
15. I stood _____ earshot.	o. top

Q26. Finish up these common American phrases:

1. I live a stone's _____ from you.
2. She came apart at the _____.
3. It went in one _____ and out the other.
4. He was in the wrong _____ at the wrong time.
5. I got paid under the _____.
6. He ran off with his _____ between his legs.
7. You can't keep a good _____ down.
8. They're somewhere between the _____ and the deep blue sea.
9. We wandered off the beaten _____.
10. She went out on a _____ for her friend.
11. You're barking up the wrong _____.
12. I hit the target smack _____ in the middle.

On the ball, on the house

13. I'd like my _____ over easy.
14. You're really scraping the bottom of the _____.
15. That job's right up my _____.

Q27. Here are some more easy ones:

1. I got a little _____ tracked.   a. out
2. We'll need to hunker _____.   b. around
3. I'll bend over _____ for you.   c. at
4. She made it _____ scratch.   d. side
5. This is strictly _____ the record.   e. through
6. We held them _____ bay.   f. against
7. I've got the _____ track on that job.   g. down
8. _____ my dead body!   h. in
9. He's not going to wait _____ any longer.   i. backwards
10. They've hit rock _____.   j. off
11. The prices went _____ the roof.   k. on
12. It looks like our backs are _____ the wall. l. inside
13. She had me _____ stitches.   m. from
14. What _____ earth are you doing?   n. over
15. He spoke _____ of turn.   o. bottom

Q28. Use location words to select commands.

1. It's late, so why don't you turn _____.   a. around
2. It's cramped, so scoot _____.   b. ahead
3. It's noisy, so settle _____.   c. in
4. It's moving, so hop _____.   d. through
5. It's over, so take _____.   e. back
6. It's empty, so fill it _____.   f. over
7. It's ready, so full steam _____.   g. on
8. It's dangerous, so stay _____.   h. up
9. It's lost, so look _____.   i. down
10. It's unfinished, so see it _____.   j. off

Answers

Q25 1. j   2. o   3. l   4. n   5. m   6. a   7. c   8. i   9. k   10. e
11. h   12. f   13. d   14. b   15. g

Q26. 1. throw   2. seams   3. ear   4. place   5. table   6. tail   7. man
8. devil   9. track   10. limb   11. tree   12. dab   13. eggs
14. barrel   15. alley

Q27. 1. d   2. g   3. i   4. m   5. j   6. c   7. l   8. n   9. b   10. o
11. e   12. f   13. h   14. k   15. a

Q28. 1. c   2. f   3. i   4. g   5. j   6. h   7. b   8. e   9. a   10. d

Give yourself 1 point for every correct answer:

A LITTLE HISTORY

- To have someone **over a barrel** is to leave them helpless or at a great disadvantage. Apparently, American pioneers believed that once you pulled a drowning person from the river, it was necessary to lay them stomach first over a barrel to drain out all the water from the lungs. Needless to say, this technique is not encouraged today.
- During country squirrel hunts, the key was to scare the animals up a small isolated tree, and then force them to climb **out on a limb**. At such a vulnerable location, the exposed creatures became easy targets for even children with sticks or stones. Today, the expression carries a similar meaning for humans, where one is left out in the open, in danger, or at risk.
- As America grew during the Industrial Age, craftsmen, architects, and engineers worked on their construction plans by hand, which meant that all miscalculations or changes in the designs had to **go back to the drawing board**. Nowadays, we use the expression anytime we've failed in an enterprise and have to start over again.

BORN IN THE U.S.A.

- Numerous phrases in all-American English refer to downward movement, perhaps describing life in more difficult times:

   *When the chips are **down**, we need to **get down** to work.
   If we **lay down** the law, it's all **downhill** from here.*

- Speaking of downward movement:

   *You can bet your **bottom** dollar, we need to get to the **bottom** of this. And that's the **bottom** line.*

? ON YOUR OWN

1. *Do you have any **skeletons in your closet**?*
2. *Have you ever **been in a pickle**?*
3. *When would you use, "**Bottoms up**"?*
4. *What was the last thing you **heard through the grapevine**?*

Q29. This time, connect each location phrase with its proper definition:

1. naked	a. in a nutshell
2. sluggish	b. in the black
3. single file	c. in a dead heat
4. uninformed	d. in a pinch
5. well-known	e. in the red
6. to summarize	f. in nothing flat
7. disoriented	g. in poor taste
8. tied	h. in the dark
9. tight spot	i. in the spotlight
10. vulgar	j. in the buff
11. written	k. in a tizzy
12. very fast	l. in the cards
13. the future	m. in the doldrums
14. with debt	n. in black and white
15. without debt	o. in tandem

Q30. Plenty of phrases include the word **on**:

1. on the same page	a. for free
2. on the fritz	b. doing well
3. on the level	c. healing
4. on the double	d. for sale
5. on the ball	e. tight budget
6. on the back burner	f. punctual
7. on a bender	g. honestly
8. on a shoestring	h. in agreement
9. on pins and needles	i. for later
10. on the air	j. no drinking

11. on the block   k. anxiously
12. on the dot   l. broken
13. on the house   m. broadcasting
14. on the mend   n. drunken spree
15. on the wagon   o. faster

Q31. What's the BEST way to complete the following?

1. Her husband's   a. in the bag
2. You get   b. on the table
3. You're my ace   c. on the carpet
4. I got called   d. in the pink
5. Put all your cards   e. on his nerves
6. Help someone   f. in the wash
7. The guard has to stay   g. in the doghouse
8. She's feeling   h. in the hole
9. It will all come out   i. in a jam
10. This game is   j. on his toes

Answers

Q29. 1. j   2. m   3. o   4. h
        5. i   6. a   7. k   8. c
        9. d   10. g   11. n   12. f
        13. l   14. e   15. b
Q30. 1. h   2. l   3. g   4. o   5. b
        6. i   7. n   8. e   9. k   10. m
        11. d   12. f   13. a   14. c   15. j
Q31. 1. g   2. e   3. h   4. c   5. b   6. i   7. j   8. d   9. f   10. a

The early bird
catches the worm

Give yourself 1 point for every correct answer:

A LITTLE HISTORY

- In American homes with servants, masters verbally chastised their employees by calling them **on the carpet** in the main hallway. Not only were the other employees able to hear the reprimand, but other family members were also informed of what went wrong and why.

- Many believe that the expression, **in the pink** comes from the garden flower of the genus *Dianthus*, which is bright pink when in full bloom. Over time, the phrase has come to mean that somebody is in the best of health.
- The phrase **on the wagon**, which refers to abstaining from alcoholic beverages, originally referred to the water wagons used to spray the dusty roads of American cities. Obviously, if you are on the water wagon, you are not at the saloon.

BORN IN THE U.S.A.

- One forgets the myriad of all-American words and expressions we use every day without thinking.

    Ellen likes the burger joint and pool hall at the strip mall, while Susan prefers her local bridge club and sewing circle downtown.

SAY IT RIGHT

- Remember that some one-liners have more than one meaning.

    I left my mountain bike on the rocks, my marriage is on the rocks, and that's my bourbon on the rocks!

- And location words are often used as descriptions.

    Coaches have found across the board that players who are over the hill run out of gas sooner.

ON YOUR OWN

1. *Have you ever visited the **city pound**, **skid row**, or an **outhouse**?*
2. *Name something you've **swept under the rug**.*
3. *Have you ever **been up in arms**?*

WORDS OF WISDOM

"Speak softly and carry a big stick; you will go far."

Theodore Roosevelt

X. SAY WHEN!

Q32. After talking about location words, we need to chat about when
things take place. Work on the following words and one-liners
dealing with time:

1. Long time no _____ .   S _____
2. _____ upon a time . . . .   O _____
3. A _____ in time saves nine.   S _____
4. Time is of the _____.   E _____
5. There's no time like the _____.   P _____
6. Time _____ for no man.   W _____
7. He got here in the _____ of time.   N _____
8. I had the time of my _____.   L _____
9. She's living on _____ time.   B _____
10. That's how they pass the time of _____. D _____

Q33. Pick the word that relates to **when**:

1. It's no _____ said than done.   a. once
2. The _____ bird catches the worm.   b. dawn
3. Let's finish it _____ and for all.   c. midnight
4. It's all in a _____'s work.   d. night
5. This is your _____ of truth.   e. early
6. It's just a fly-by- _____ romance.   f. daylight
7. Well, it's better _____ than ever.   g. moment
8. She was burning the _____ oil.   h. day
9. He was walking around like that in broad _____. i. sooner
10. Let's meet at the crack of _____.   j. late

Answers

Q32. 1. see   2. Once   3. stitch   4. essence   5. present   6. waits
       7. nick   8. life   9. borrowed   10. day

Q33. 1. i   2. e   3. a   4. h   5. g   6. d   7. j   8. c   9. f   10. b

Give yourself 1 point for every correct answer:

A LITTLE HISTORY

- The very first **Memorial Day** was actually called Decoration Day, and it began in the town of Waterloo, New York. In 1868, Retired Major General Jonathan A. Logan led Civil War veterans in a march through town to the cemetery, where friends and families gathered to decorate military graves with flowers.

- The expression **fly-by-night** is from the 1600s, when it described the undependable and erratic behavior of an elderly woman, especially if she was considered a witch. Today it generally refers to any business that opens, makes money quickly, and then suddenly disappears.

- A **moment of truth**, which refers to any crisis point or time of decision in a person's life, is thought to come from Spain, where a bullfighter would eventually have to decide when it was best to plunge his sword into the animal. Early writings show that this was often called *el momento de la verdad*.

Throw the baby out with the bathwater

BORN IN THE U.S.A.

- The fact that we are a **time**-oriented society is proved by hundreds of expressions:

> *Time's up, my friend, so let's talk **some other time**. For the time being, there's no **wasting time**, and personally, I've got **no time to kill**. It's **high time** you learned that no matter the **time zone**, here in this country, **time flies**.*

*Depending upon where you live in the U.S., sunrise can be referred to as **dawn, sun-up**, or **daybreak**. Sunset, on the other hand, is usually called **nightfall, sundown**, or **dusk**.*

ON YOUR OWN

Can you name the month when we celebrate these?

1. ***Dr. King's Birthday*** _____
2. ***Memorial Day*** _____
3. ***Veteran's Day*** _____
4. ***Groundhog Day*** _____
5. ***Arbor Day*** _____

WORDS OF WISDOM

"Early to bed, early to rise, makes a man healthy, wealthy, and wise."

Benjamin Franklin

ALL-AMERICAN CROSSWORD 2

Across

5. No can _____.
7. I hear you loud and _____.
8. He's sowing his _____ oats.
9. We're _____ a roll!
10. It's _____ sealed.
12. How now brown _____?
13. We stood ____ attention.
14. They're like two peas in a _____.
16. _____ and Roebuck.
19. _____ I had a hammer... .
20. Did you check the want _____?
21. I'm _____ the mood for love... .
22. He's feeling a little _____ and out.
23. She got _____ of him.

Down

1. That's my _____ in the hole.
2. You'll have to _____ your license.
3. She had to _____ for the test.
4. I _____ out in the dentist's chair.
5. It's on my "to _____" list.
6. If you _____ knew!
8. Potty-trained kids don't _____ their beds.
10. It's too _____ to handle.

11. They stayed till the bitter _____.
12. He's a real _____ shark.
14. You could hear a _____ drop.
15. What ____ it?
16. Don't be such a ____ sack.
17. ____ the World Turns.
18. There's no time to _____ on your hands.

A finished crossword is on page 241.

A finished crossword is on page 241.

Q34. **When did you say?**

1. I haven't seen you in a _____ of Sundays.
2. That'll be the _____.
3. Thank goodness it's _____.
4. She went to _____ School every week.
5. Here _____, gone tomorrow.
6. It's either _____ or never.
7. We decided on the spur of the _____.
8. It happens only _____ in a blue moon.
9. I'll love you _____ and a day.
10. He scared the living _____ out of her.

a. forever
b. once
c. moment
d. month
e. daylights
f. today
g. Sunday
h. now
i. Friday
j. day

Q35. **And these two-word expressions must be unscrambled first:**

1. night
2. blue
3. sun
4. dooms
5. leap
6. Sunday
7. tea
8. never
9. hour
10. minute

a. DNHA
b. EMTI
c. NALD
d. DAMOYN
e. SLASG
f. LOW
g. ADY
h. WNOD
i. ERAY
j. VRRDIE

Scratch my back and I'll
scratch yours

Q36. Stay in season, as you connect words that fit together BEST:

1. April	a. bride
2. spring	b. leaves
3. October	c. day
4. Yule	d. fest
5. June	e. green
6. August	f. camp
7. May	g. tide
8. summer	h. cleaning
9. autumn	i. moon
10. winter	j. fools

Q37. And how's the weather?

1. He's just a fair _____ friend.	a. sun
2. I'm going to have to take a _____ check.	b. storm
3. Everything at work is starting to _____ .	c. thunder
4. I need to catch my second _____.	d. weather
5. She called me everything under the _____.	e. moon
6. I don't know him from the man in the _____.	f. snowball
7. Let's try to stem the _____.	g. cloud
8. We think there's a _____ brewing between them.	h. wind
9. I don't want to steal your _____.	i. rain
10. She's under a _____ of suspicion.	j. tide

Answers

Q34. 1. d   2. j   3. i   4. g   5. f   6. h   7. c   8. b   9. a   10. e
Q35. 1. f (owl)   2. d (Monday)   3. h (down)   4. g (day)   5. i (year)
     6. j (driver)   7. b (time)   8. c (land)   9. e (glass)   10. a (hand)
Q36. 1. j   2. h   3. d   4. g   5. a   6. i   7. c   8. f   9. b   10. e
Q37. 1. d   2. i   3. f   4. h   5. a   6. e   7. j   8. b   9. c   10. g

__Give yourself 1 point for every correct answer:__ _____

A LITTLE HISTORY

- For years in France, New Year's Day was celebrated on April 1. Once the date was officially changed to January 1, some people still called out New Year's greeting to their friends in April. These folks were considered **fools**, which is why April 1 is still referred to as **April Fools Day**. The name made it to the New World, while its origins were forgotten.
- In 1709, playwright John Dennis devised a clever way to simulate the sound of thunder in one of his productions. Years later, while watching a presentation of Macbeth, the same technique was used, so he stood up and cried out, "My God, they are **stealing my thunder!**" Today, the expression carries a similar meaning, which is to take away another person's idea or claim to fame.

BORN IN THE U.S.A.

- You'll hear the word **day** in America *day in* and *day out*:

  *You say you'll do it **one of these days**, but to me it's **as clear as day**—you prefer to **daydream** about **the good old days**. Believe me, as your boss on the **day shift**, your days are numbered!*

ON YOUR OWN

1. *Define **daylight saving time**, **April showers**, and **spring fever**.*
2. *You saw **holly** at Christmas, but what flower did you see on Easter?*
3. *Have you ever **been under the weather**?*

WORDS OF WISDOM

"I never think of the future; it comes soon enough."

Albert Einstein

WHAT'S MY SCORE?

TOTAL CORRECT: _____

TOTAL POSSIBLE: ___449___

Chapter Three

Small Talk

XI. PICK A NUMBER!

Q1. In any conversation, someone will always make reference to a number or two. Check these:

1. He was _____ sheets to the wind.	a. two
2. It looks like he's batting _____.	b. ten
3. She's on cloud _____.	c. four
4. You're really behind the _____ ball now.	d. six
5. It's Snow White and the _____ dwarfs.	e. one
6. He's got a _____-track mind.	f. nine
7. They're like _____ peas in a pod.	g. zero
8. People called in from the _____ corners of the earth.	h. seven
9. We used to go shopping at the local five & _____ .	i. eight
10. Give me _____ of one and a half dozen of the other.	j. three

Q2. Now connect those phrases that relate BEST:

1. the three Rs	a. not 20-20
2. forty winks	b. headwear
3. one-two	c. kitty cat
4. three rings	d. over and out
5. nine lives	e. a quarter
6. two left feet	f. nap time
7. ten-four	g. the big top
8. four eyes	h. buckle my shoe
9. ten-gallon	i. school days
10. two bits	j. dance lessons

Q3. Here are some more, but who's counting?

1. _____'s a crowd	a. thousand
2. He always tries to be _____ up on you.	b. six
3. Let me tell you a thing or _____.	c. twelve
4. She looks like a _____ dollars.	d. ten
5. Hindsight's always twenty- _____.	e. million
6. The baby gets around on all _____'s.	f. one
7. I wouldn't touch it with a _____ -foot pole.	g. twenty

8. The old cowboy took out his _____-gun.   h. two
9. We read about Jesus and the _____ disciples.   i. three
10. If I've told you once, I've told you a _____ times.   j. four

Answers

Q1. 1. j   2. g   3. f   4. i   5. h   6. e   7. a   8. c   9. b   10. d
Q2. 1. i   2. f   3. h   4. g   5. c   6. j   7. d   8. a   9. b   10. e
Q3. 1. i   2. f   3. h   4. e   5. g   6. j   7. d   8. b   9. c   10. a

Give yourself 1 point for every correct answer: _____

A LITTLE HISTORY

- **On cloud nine** refers to the ninth of the ten heavens in Dante's *Paradise*, where one was placed very close to Divine presence. Obviously, being in that position would leave one feeling euphoric, which is precisely what the expression means today.
- Gold and silver coins once served as currency in America. To spend less than the value of the coin, it was often cut into pieces or bits, which were usually halves, quarters, and eighths. This is where **pieces of eight** come from, along with the old phrase for a quarter, **two bits**.

SAY IT RIGHT

- Be frank, did you know that the following words should be hyphenated?

    I double-checked, and **the double-crosser double-parked.**

ON YOUR OWN

1. *Explain **catch-22** and **23-skidoo**.*
2. *Where might you hear, **Take five?***
3. *When will your **number be up?***

Q4.   BEST answers only, please:

1. Guys like that are a dime a _____.	a. pair
2. That was a _____-hearted attempt.	b. seventh
3. He gave her the _____ degree.	c. zero
4. They drank a _____ of gin.	d. double
5. She's in _____ heaven.	e. half
6. I don't want to play _____ fiddle to anyone.	f. first
7. Let's try to _____ in on the problem.	g. dozen
8. He needs a new _____ of trousers.	h. fifth
9. I want you to get here on the _____.	i. third
10. It was love at _____ sight.	j. second

Q5.   Match words with their meanings for these next expressions:

1. A-one	a. pipsqueak
2. the old one-two	b. disposed
3. three-legged	c. a good deal
4. fifty-fifty	d. boogie down
5. umpteenth	e. the best
6. zilch	f. race
7. two-step	g. countless
8. baker's dozen	h. nada
9. half-pint	i. a punch
10. eighty-six	j. Dutch treat

Q6.   Here are a few numbers that every American should remember.

1. The U.S. flag has _____ stripes.
2. There are currently _____ states in the U.S.A.
3. The U.S. has _____ levels of government.
4. One must be _____ years old to vote in America.
5. Americans vote for a President every _____ years.

How about some important numbers in U.S. history:

6. Columbus discovered America in the year _____.
7. The Declaration of Independence was signed in _____.
8. The _____ amendment guaranteed women the right to vote.

9. George Washington was America's _____ president.
10. Martin Luther King's birthday is celebrated each year on the _____ Monday in January.

Answers

Q4. 1. g   2. e   3. i   4. h   5. b
    6. j   7. c   8. a   9. d   10. f
Q5. 1. e   2. i   3. f   4. j   5. g
    6. h   7. d   8. c   9. a   10. b
Q6. 1. thirteen   2. fifty
    3. three   4. eighteen
    5. four   6. 1492
    7. 1776   8. 19th
    9. 1st   10. 3rd

Two-faced liar

Give yourself 1 point for every correct answer: _____

BORN IN THE U.S.A.

• Here is a simple, all-American success story. Can you understand everything?

> *We literally went **from rags to riches**. Once, we were so **strapped** that we couldn't **make ends meet**. After we **forked out** all we had **to pay the piper**, we started **to scrimp** and save every **sawbuck** we earned. When we had **cash to burn**, we didn't throw it away. I was **tight-fisted** and **held onto the purse strings**, so we always **got our money's worth** and never paid for anything **through the nose**. We've learned that it really pays **to save for a rainy day**.*

ON YOUR OWN

1. *Have you ever seen a **one-man band**?*
2. *Have you ever gone **the whole nine yards**?*
3. *Finish this: **One for the money, two for the show, three ...***

A LITTLE HISTORY

- **The whole nine yards** is the total number of sails that could be raised on a ship under the best sailing conditions. There were usually three masts, with each mast holding three square sails. The horizontal stays that supported the sails were called yards. When at full speed, the vessel was said to have taken **the whole nine yards**. Today, the phrase refers to completing a quality job, without cutting any corners.

- To become a Freemason, one must pass through various degrees of proficiency. By the time one reaches level three, the evaluation becomes a bit more difficult or severe. Today, to be given the **third degree** simply means to be intensely questioned or reprimanded.

- The Roman god Janus had two faces, supposedly in order to keep better guard at the gates of heaven. However, the expression **two-faced** comes from the old phrase, **double-faced**, which means being deceitful or trying to head in two directions at the same time.

- The sights on a gun or cannon originally consisted of a horizontal line with a series of numbers above it. To aim correctly, the key was to line up the number zero by adjusting the sights. Over time, **to zero in on something** has developed a much broader definition, and now it means to focus, aim, or set sights on anything at all.

WORDS OF WISDOM

"Genius is one per cent inspiration, ninety-nine per cent perspiration."

Thomas Alva Edison

XII. TAKE A LETTER!

*Q*7. Now that we're done with numbers, find out how many letters you know:

1. I have to give you an _____ for effort.   a. Y
2. Jimmy was in the backyard shooting off his B-_____ gun.   b. G
3. They don't know about it, so let's keep it on the _____-T.   c. Z
4. You'll have to mind your _____'s and Q's.   d. T

5. She needed some exercise, so she went to the _____.   e. B
6. He's in the bedroom catching some _____'s.   f. R
7. We had to go down the street and make a _____-turn.   g. Q
8. I had nothing on but a _____-string.   h. A
9. His nickname suits him to a _____.   i. P
10. After this project, you're going to need a little R & _____.   j. U

Q8. This time, use two letters to fill in the blanks:

1. If you keep take taking those pills, you might _____.   a. P.E.
2. Put on your _____'s, and get ready for bed.   b. P.D.
3. She has the highest _____ of any student I've ever had.   c. O.D.
4. We learned about _____ in our sexual health class today.   d. P.O.
5. That restroom is out of _____.   e. O.K.
6. They had to hook up the patient to an _____.   f. I.Q.
7. His father is a captain in the local _____.   g. V.D.
8. Did you send the package to my _____ Box?   h. I.V.
9. Everything turned out A-_____.   i. T.P.
10. Susie got a good grade in her _____ class.   j. P.J.

Q9. These need three or four letters, but you'll have to unscramble them first:

1. I'll try to get there _____.   a. NTT
2. The show was so popular that there was _____.   b. OUF
3. She got to sit in the _____ section with the bigwigs.   c. VSPR
4. This is the _____ that he wrote you for the loan.   d. IRP
5. All the guys sat around in their _____'s.   e. PVI
6. Did you fill out the _____ for the wedding?   f. VBD
7. We don't believe in alien beings or _____'s.   g. CAB
8. They blew up the cave with _____.   h. UIO
9. This job is as easy as _____.   i. ROS
10. The words on his gravestone read _____.   j. SAAP

Answers

Q7.   1. h   2. e   3. g   4. i   5. a   6. c   7. j   8. b   9. d   10. f
Q8.   1. c   2. j   3. f   4. g   5. i   6. h   7. b   8. d   9. e   10. a
Q9.   1. j (ASAP)   2. i (SRO)   3. e (VIP)   4. h (IOU)   5. f (BVD)
        6. c (RSVP)   7. b (UFO)   8. a (TNT)   9. g (ABC)   10. d (RIP)

Give yourself 1 point for every correct answer: _____

A LITTLE HISTORY

- Barkeeps in old taverns used to mark how much each person drank on a chalkboard, often writing *P* for pint and *Q* for quart. Patrons who kept drinking were often told to **Mind their Ps and Qs**, so that they wouldn't run up a tab that couldn't be paid.

- **A-OK** was first used by John A. Powers, of NASA, as he commented on a manned flight back in 1961, letting the media know that all aspects of the mission were under control. The phrase caught on, and has been used since to express that things are fine, or that everything is going well.

Catching Zs

BORN IN THE U.S.A.

- Acronyms are an American favorite.

    *Let's see, it's **BYOB** for the **TGIF** party.*
    *He's got **BO** and needs to take a shower **PDQ**.*
    *Ah, forget it—I'll just sit at the **PC**, eat **M&Ms**, and check out these **DVDs**.*

- The letter *X* has been used as a signature for those who cannot read or write. Here are a few other examples:

    *Look at this map—**X** marks the spot.*
    *You'll have to **X**-out the incorrect answers.*
    *I don't know all the **Xs** and **Os** of football.*

ON YOUR OWN

Have you ever written these in a note or letter? Spell them out!

Jr. _____	*Bros.* _____	*Ms.* _____
i.e. _____	*Supt.* _____	*ea.* _____
P.S. _____	*AKA* _____	*etc.* _____

Q10. Acronyms, eh? In the following activity, connect each title with its correct definition:

1.	REP	a.	loves animals
2.	DA	b.	did hard time
3.	MC	c.	assists MDs
4.	RN	d.	is a head honcho
5.	REF	e.	works in a courtroom
6.	CON	f.	does taxes
7.	MP	g.	loves the mike
8.	CPA	h.	is in sales
9.	CEO	i.	calls fouls
10.	VET	j.	is a soldier cop

Q11. Now connect the abbreviations or acronyms that match up BEST:

1.	PVT.	a.	NBC
2.	INC.	b.	JFK
3.	RFD	c.	NATO
4.	OAC	d.	HT.
5.	OZ.	e.	NBA
6.	CBS	f.	COD
7.	AFL	g.	CO.
8.	DEM	h.	QT.
9.	WT.	i.	YR.
10.	WK.	j.	CIO
11.	UN	k.	GOP
12.	NFL	l.	SGT.
13.	LAX	m.	APR
14.	FBI	n.	PhD
15.	MBA	o.	CIA

Chasing the rainbow

Q12. Read the key word, and then find the letters that relate:

1.	BOXING	a.	RPM
2.	TEACHERS	b.	USDA
3.	MEAT	c.	AKA
4.	BOAT	d.	PDST
5.	AIRPORTS	e.	AAA
6.	NICKNAME	f.	AP
7.	NEWS	g.	PTA
8.	ENGINE	h.	FAA
9.	TIME	i.	TKO
10.	CLUB	j.	USS

Q13. Which words relate BEST to these businesses, organizations, or agencies:

1.	PETS	a.	USMC
2.	CARS	b.	FCC
3.	SPORTS	c.	NAACP
4.	STOCKS	d.	NASA
5.	BORDERS	e.	NYSE
6.	MOVIES	f.	UAW
7.	SOLDIERS	g.	NCAA
8.	SPACE	h.	SPCA
9.	RADIO/TV	i.	MGM
10.	CIVIL RIGHTS	j.	INS

Answers

Q10. 1. h   2. e   3. g   4. c   5. i   6. b   7. j   8. f   9. d   10. a

Q11. 1. l   2. g   3. f   4. m   5. h   6. a   7. j   8. k   9. d   10. i
    11. c   12. e   13. b   14. o   15. n

Q12. 1. i   2. g   3. b   4. j   5. h   6. c   7. f   8. a   9. d   10. e

Q13. 1. h   2. f   3. g   4. e   5. j   6. i   7. a   8. d   9. b   10. c

Give yourself 1 point for every correct answer:

BORN IN THE U.S.A.

- Americans everywhere try hard to keep it short:

The GI went AWOL.	*He's a PR guy for Smith Bros.*
D-day was in WWII.	*I'll be VP by X-mas.*
They scored a TD in OT.	*There's an S.O.S. on the A.P.B.*

ON YOUR OWN

1. *Can you name each category for the three lists below?*

   St., Ave., Rd., Blvd., Ln.   _____

   in., ft., yd., mi., cm.   _____

   CA, PA, GA, MA, WA   _____

2. *Do you need the three **Rs** to join a **4-H** Club? And can a person be declared **4-F** because of the **D-Ts**?*

3. *Have you ever had a **BLT** or a **PB&J** with some **OJ**? By the way, do you own any old **LPs**?*

A LITTLE HISTORY

- For several years, the letters **G.I.** simply meant **government issue**, so U.S. soldiers used the phrase in reference to the equipment they received. Over time, however, it became clear that the soldiers were government property, too, so **G.I.** became synonymous with anyone who marched off to fight for his or her country.

- The international radio signal for distress, **S.O.S.**, was chosen because the letters in Morse code were distinctive and easy to produce. The letters stand for either **Save Our Souls** or **Save Our Ship**, and were first sent out in 1908 from the American ship, *Azaoahe*.

WORDS OF WISDOM

"Wisdom is made up of ten parts, nine of which are silence."

Unknown

XIII. AND?

Q14. Folks in the U.S. tend to combine words and phrases to get their point across. Let's test your proficiency with & expressions.

1. Let's keep it _____ & sweet.
2. Your father told you time & _____.
3. You'll just have to grin & _____ it.
4. It was nip & _____ for quite awhile.
5. Don't give me that song & _____ routine.
6. All they lived on was bread & _____.
7. Now I'm _____ & fancy free.
8. The best jobs are _____ & far between.
9. I'm not interested in another _____ & pony show.
10. You can't just pick & _____.

Q15. Keep filling in the first word that comes to mind:

1. It's all touch & _____ from here.
2. You look all bright-eyed & _____!
3. The boat was rocking _____ & fro.
4. They were fighting tooth & _____.
5. It was raining cats & _____.
6. There was a lot of _____ & go traffic.
7. She learned by trial & _____.
8. Everyone got there _____ & sound.
9. That guy loves to wheel & _____.
10. He left the kitchen _____ & span.

Q16. And these are simple commands:

1. Okay, up and _____!
2. Rise and _____!
3. _____ and get it!
4. Front and _____!
5. Over and _____!

Answers

Q14. 1. short   2. again   3. bear
4. tuck   5. dance   6. water
7. footloose   8. few   9. dog
10. choose

Q15. 1. go   2. bushy-tailed   3. to
4. nail   5. dogs   6. stop
7. error   8. safe   9. deal
10. spic

Q16. 1. at 'em   2. shine   3. Come
4. center   5. out

Give yourself 1 point for every correct answer:

Raining cats and dogs

A LITTLE HISTORY

- Centuries ago, there was a common expression, **short and sweet, like a donkey's gallop**, which meant that something turned out better than expected. In other words, the experience was brief, but quite pleasant. Over the years, the phrase was trimmed, but it has kept a similar meaning.
- The story goes that during World War I, a U.S. pilot flew into base with a badly damaged wing. When asked how he made it, the soldier responded how he'd been praying all the way to safety. Someone then replied, "So, you made it on one wing and a prayer!" Today, **a wing and a prayer** means that the situation is hopeful, but not very likely to succeed.
- **Spic and span**, which means very clean and in good order, comes from the ancient phrase, **spike and span new**. A **spike** was a nail, and a **span** was a wooden chip, so shiny nails and polished wood became known as spic and span. Nowadays, the expression simply refers to being extremely neat or clean.

SAY IT RIGHT

- Many one-liners have a repeated pattern:

> **Is everything on the up and up?**
> **That guy's a dirty so and so.**
> **We were doing such and such.**
> **It happened to me again and again.**
> **She was driving round and round.**

BORN IN THE U.S.A.

- More insights into the U.S. culture? Fill in the blanks:

> *This country has been called the **land of milk and _____**.*
> *He took his money to the **savings and _____**.*
> *Firefighters drive **hook and _____** trucks.*

ON YOUR OWN

1. *Explain the expression, **tar and feathered**.*
2. *Do you enjoy a good **cloak and dagger** story?*
3. *Do you know the **ins and outs** of the U.S. government?*

Q17. Unscramble the letters, and then fill in the blanks:

1. I love you with all my heart and _____.	a. WHA
2. She stood head and _____ above all the rest.	b. SIMS
3. He likes to hem and _____ throughout his speech.	c. AEHDT
4. You left me _____ and dry out there.	d. YRD
5. It was a _____ and run accident.	e. NHET
6. I always hunt and _____ whenever I type.	f. OLUS
7. Looking for work here is usually hit or _____.	g. DEORHSUSL
8. They drop by every now and _____.	h. KECP
9. That was a very cut and _____ presentation.	i. THI
10. She said it's a matter of life and _____.	j. IGHH

Q18. No answers provided here!

1. He was my own flesh and _____.
2. They've been through thick and _____.
3. I promise to love you in sickness and in _____.
4. Don't start acting all _____ and mighty.
5. The ruling was fair and _____.
6. _____ and stones can break my bones, but words can never hurt me.
7. A good marriage involves a lot of give and _____.
8. She used to be a famous rock and _____ star.
9. I guess I'll have to _____ and puff my way up all those stairs.
10. They gave us plenty of hugs and _____ at the airport.

Q19. Now, instead of **and**, express yourself with **or**. One letter will get you started:

1. I'll get around to it **s**_____ or **l**_____.
2. Flip the coin and call it **h**_____ or **t**_____!
3. We'll bring in that outlaw, **d**_____ or **a**_____.
4. That's my final offer—**t**_____ it or **l**_____ it.
5. Well, tough guy, are you a **m**_____ or a **m**_____?
6. They'll find a way, by **h**_____ or by **c**_____.
7. This mission must be accomplished—**d**_____ or **d**_____.
8. There's no **r**_____ or **r**_____ why she should act that way.
9. He never knows if he's **c**_____ or **g**_____.
10. Sorry, no ifs, **a**_____, or **b**_____ about it.

Answers

Q17. 1. f   2. g   3. a   4. j   5. i   6. h   7. b   8. e   9. d   10. c
Q18. 1. blood   2. thin   3. health   4. high   5. square   6. Sticks
       7. take   8. roll   9. huff   10. kisses
Q19. 1. sooner, later   2. heads, tails   3. dead, alive   4. take, leave
       5. man, mouse   6. hook, crook   7. do, die   8. rhyme, reason
       9. coming, going   10. ands, buts

Give yourself 1 point for every correct answer:

A LITTLE HISTORY

• During the early 1800s, American pioneers often **cut and dried** their meats, skins, fruit, herbs, flowers, and even lumber in order to prepare for tough times or bad weather. The expression is still used today to describe anything that is prepared beforehand or routine.

• As early American trailblazers rode horseback through shrubbery, at times the foliage was so thick that they had to stop and cut their way through. At other times, they came across open spaces, with only thin patches of undergrowth to clear. Once their journey was complete, many of these daring pioneers would comment how they had been **through thick and thin**. We now use the expression to support one's persistence or ability to overcome life's ups and downs.

Couch potato

ON YOUR OWN

See if you can create sentences with the following:

1. **sink or swim:** _____

2. **friend or foe:** _____

3. **like it or lump it:** _____

4. **feast or famine:** _____

5. **for better or for worse:** _____

BORN IN THE U.S.A.

- Some famous duos stand out in U.S. entertainment history:

    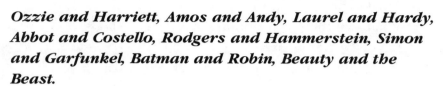

    Ozzie and Harriett, Amos and Andy, Laurel and Hardy, Abbot and Costello, Rodgers and Hammerstein, Simon and Garfunkel, Batman and Robin, Beauty and the Beast.

WORDS OF WISDOM

"And so, my fellow Americans, ask not what your country can do for you; ask what you can do for your country."

John F. Kennedy

XIV. CHIT-CHAT!

Q20. What does it sound like when folks in the U.S. sit around shooting the breeze? This next set contains classic exchanges that people use every day:

1. Hello **there**.
2. What have you been _____ to?
3. Well, _____ who's here!
4. We seem to keep _____ into each other.
5. I've been _____ to call you.
6. Life _____ be better!
7. Been staying out of _____!
8. _____ as a clam!
9. Been keeping my _____ clean!
10. _____ and dandy!
11. Been up to no _____, as usual.

Q21. Now finish up these expressions that contain the word, **what**:

1. What in the _____ are you doing?
2. What's the _____ idea?
3. What's all the _____ about?
4. I'll _____ you what.
5. We found pencils, pens, and what _____ you in the desk.
6. It's taking me forever to learn what's _____.
7. _____ what! It's none of my business.
8. What do you _____ we go over to Mary's house?
9. You've got what it _____ to be great player.
10. What's the _____ with him today?

a. what
b. takes
c. so
d. say
e. world
f. have
g. tell
h. matter
i. big
j. fuss

Answers

Q20. 2. up   3. look   4. bumping   5. meaning   6. couldn't
   7. trouble   8. Happy   9. nose   10. Fine   11. good
Q21. 1. e   2. i   3. j   4. g   5. f   6. a   7. c   8. d   9. b   10. h

__Give yourself 1 point for every correct answer:__

A LITTLE HISTORY

- In New England, it is still customary to dig up clams buried in the sand at low tide, which is why the old expression, **Happy as a clam at high tide** made sense. However, over the years it has been shortened to merely **Happy as a clam**, which actually sounds a little strange.

- The phrase **fine and dandy** is from eighteenth century England, and it describes a well-dressed person of high society. A **dandy** referred to a neatly dressed gentlemen who wore **fine** clothes. Today, the expression simply means that everything seems to be going well.

ON YOUR OWN

• *Describe a situation where these might come in handy:*

1. **What's good for the goose...**
2. **What's a nice girl like you...?**
3. **What you don't know...**

ALL-AMERICAN CROSSWORD 3

Across

2. Scary movies give me the _____.
5. It'll all come out in the _____.
7. She's locked up in the nut _____.
10. Put ___ or shut ___!
12. (means strange or foreign)
13. Let's go to the mini_____.
16. That lousy firecracker was a _____!
17. (means ruffian or rowdy)

Down

1. _____ and Pa Kettle.
2. _____ done it?
3. Let's all chip ___.
4. (means sloppy or careless)
6. He's a real square _____.

8. Can you _____ up a tree?
9. Looks like a ___ is brewing.
11. I just had my _____ teeth pulled.
14. They go to mass on ____ Wednesday.
15. It takes _____ to tango.

A finished crossword is on page 242.

Q22. What's more, here's more ***what***. Choose from the list below:

1. Well, look what the _____ dragged in!
2. What on _____ is that?
3. I can't figure out what makes her _____.
4. So what are you driving _____?
5. What _____ is new?
6. And what _____ something happens?
7. What'd you _____ me?
8. My grandpa used to give my dad something called "what-_____."
9. What's the weather _____ today?
10. I just saw old what's-his- _____ from high school.

Q23. Speaking of one-liners, try these expressions of agreement:

1. You're darn _____!   a. say
2. You've said a _____!   b. tell
3. You've got _____ there!   c. that
4. I'll _____!   d. tootin'
5. You said _____!   e. more
6. You took the _____ out of my mouth!   f. exactly
7. You can say _____ again!   g. mouthful
8. My sentiments _____!   h. it
9. You _____ 'em!   i. something
10. I couldn't agree with you _____!   j. words

Q24. Connect each phrase with the BEST definition:

1. You bet.   a. I'm laughing too hard.
2. You ain't seen nothing yet. b. I'm a little surprised.
3. You're killing me.   c. I'm in agreement.
4. You don't say.   d. I'm not in agreement.
5. Says you.   e. I'm just getting started.

Q25. Use *that* to talk about anything. Careful, *not all* these words will fit:

1. That's the last _____.
2. That's _____ biz!
3. That's the way the _____ bounces.
4. Well, how do you _____ that!
5. That's the _____ it goes!
6. That's all, _____!
7. That takes care of _____.
8. Put that in your pipe and _____ it.
9. That's the way the _____ crumbles.
10. That'll be the _____!

THAT   CAKE   HATE
LIGHT   DAY   FRIEND
STRAW   LOVE   COOKIE
NIGHT   SHOW   PLACE
TOY   LIKE   SMOKE
INHALE   BIG   WAY
MEN   FOLKS   WIND
PARTY   BALL   TIME

Answers

Q22. 1. cat 2. earth 3. tick 4. at 5. else 6. if 7. call 8. for
     9. like 10. name

Q23. 1. d 2. g 3. i 4. a 5. h 6. j 7. c 8. f 9. b 10. e

Q24. 1. c 2. e 3. a 4. b 5. d

Q25. 1. straw 2. show 3. ball 4. like 5. way 6. folks 7. that
     8. smoke 9. cookie 10. day

Give yourself 1 point for every correct answer:

A LITTLE HISTORY

- It seems that the affirmative phrase, **you bet**, is short for **you can bet your boots**, an old American expression used by miners and cowboys. During the nineteenth century, boots were invaluable to those who worked outdoors, so the only way men would **bet them** in a card game was if they held a winning hand.
- **That's the way the cookie crumbles** and **that's the way the ball bounces** entered the all-American scene around 1950, and they both imply that the results of certain events in life are unpredictable, and there's not much you can do about the past.

ON YOUR OWN

1. *When would you say **here, here** or **amen** to someone else?*
2. *Under what circumstances would you use **What's the catch?** **What's eating you?** **What of it?***
3. *Name something **that goes without saying** and **is easier said than done!***

WORDS OF WISDOM

"Good management consists of showing average people how to do the work of superior people."

John D. Rockefeller

XV. JUST DO IT!

Q26. In any conversation, people tell you what to do. Check these command phrases—can you find a match?

1. Skip it		a. Throw it away
2. Scram		b. Listen up
3. Knock it off		c. Move it
4. Stay put		d. Keep me posted
5. Shake		e. Never mind
6. Mind your own beeswax		f. Beat it
7. Let me know		g. Cut it out
8. Make it snappy		h. Butt out
9. Pay attention		i. Don't move
10. Get rid of it		j. Put her there

Q27. Now fill in the BEST command word:

1.	_____ a heart, officer. I just got my license.	a. Settle
2.	_____ off the booze. It's bad for the liver.	b. Give
3.	_____ your shirt on. I'll be with you in a moment.	c. Get
4.	_____ a sec. Something's wrong here.	d. Stick
5.	_____ your age. You're being childish.	e. Have
6.	_____ down. There's no reason to get excited.	f. Keep
7.	_____ on. I want to know what happened next.	g. Lay
8.	_____ to the point. Spare me all the details.	h. Wait
9.	_____ me a buzz later. I'll be home by six.	i. Go
10.	_____ around. There's a dance after the game.	j. Act

Q28. Take a glance at what's missing here: You should take …

1.	Take _____ a good movie.	a. over
2.	Take _____ a second job.	b. to
3.	Take _____ tennis instead of golf.	c. out
4.	Take _____ when you're ready to leave.	d. back
5.	Take _____ for me while I'm gone.	e. in
6.	Take _____ the trash.	f. down
7.	Take _____ account what I told you.	g. on
8.	Take _____ all those mean words.	h. into
9.	Take _____ this message.	i. off
10.	Take _____ heart today's sermon.	j. up

Answers

Q26. 1. e   2. f   3. g   4. i   5. j   6. h
      7. d   8. c   9. b   10. a

Q27. 1. e   2. g   3. f   4. h   5. j   6. a
      7. i   8. c   9. b   10. d

Q28. 1. e   2. g   3. j   4. i   5. a   6. c
      7. h   8. d   9. f   10. b

***Give yourself 1 point for every
correct answer:*** _____

Happy as a clam

SAY IT RIGHT

- At times, one little adverb can turn a verb into a command phrase:

    Crank it up! Suck it up! Live it up! Look it up! Talk it up!

- Most commands can be modified:

    Stay still, Be still, Sit still, Lie still, Stand still...

A LITTLE HISTORY

- *Dukes are fists, probably from the Latin word **dux**, which means **leader**, since one usually leads with the fists. **Put up your dukes** was an English slang expression for **let's fight** in the 1870s, and it became famous in the U.S. as boxing competitions gained in popularity.*
- ***Crank it up** originated in the early twentieth century as drivers of the first automobiles had to use a crank to get their engines started. The expression is used today in reference to starting any machine, but it can also mean to turn up the volume or sound.*
- *Since the 1800s, Americans have said that anyone who acts arrogantly should get **off his or her high horse**, and stop looking down on others. That is why **come off it** is still an effective way to get a person to stop behaving a certain way. It also commands someone to give up a specific idea or belief.*

ON YOUR OWN

1. *Have you ever had to **call off the dogs**?*
2. *When would you tell a person to go **suck an egg**?*
3. *Do you like to **face the facts**?*

WORDS OF WISDOM

"The secret in life is not to do what you like, but to like what you do."
Anonymous

Q29. **Put** all your effort into these; they're a little tricky:

1. Put your best foot _____.	a. into
2. Put it _____ exactly where you found it.	b. in
3. Put the camera _____ for a minute, and sit next to me.	c. back
4. Put the Christmas decorations _____ until next year.	d. off
5. Put everything you learned _____ practice.	e. on
6. Put _____ your dukes.	f. out
7. Put _____ a good word for me, please.	g. forward
8. Put _____ a happy face.	h. up
9. Put _____ the vacation until you finish the project.	i. away
10. Put _____ the fire with lots of water.	j. down

Q30. Where are you probably going to hear these instructions?

1. Book him!	a. In a cafeteria
2. Steady as she goes!	b. On a movie set
3. Press one!	c. In a garage
4. Say "ah"!	d. At a crime scene
5. Repent!	e. On a ship
6. Rev it up!	f. On an Army base
7. Hold the mayo!	g. In an exercise class
8. Fall in!	h. In a doctor's office
9. Take a lap!	i. On the telephone
10. Cut!	j. In a church

Q31. Complete this list of one-liners without any help:

1. _____ care of yourself
2. _____ me the scoop
3. _____ off the grass
4. _____ a load of her
5. _____ fly a kite
6. _____ up or shut up
7. _____ your horses
8. _____ the hay
9. _____ up or ship out
10. _____ your heart out

Disc jockey

Q32. **Come** to think of it, this command word is popular, too:

1. I hope to come _____ some money soon.	a. on
2. Can Tommy come _____ and play with us?	b. down
3. You always come _____ for me when I need help.	c. back
4. He doesn't come _____ here anymore.	d. across
5. If you do, the police will come _____ you.	e. out
6. Sometimes I come _____ with a cold.	f. around
7. I usually come _____ as a mean person.	g. into
8. Where did you come _____ with that excuse?	h. through
9. He'll come _____ from his vacations on Monday.	i. after
10. The lights didn't come _____ last night.	j. up

Answers

Q29. 1. g   2. c   3. j   4. i   5. a   6. h   7. b   8. e   9. d   10. f

Q30. 1. d   2. e   3. i   4. h   5. j   6. c   7. a   8. f   9. g   10. b

Q31. 1. take   2. give   3. keep   4. get   5. go   6. put   7. hold
         8. hit   9. shape   10. eat

Q32. 1. g   2. e   3. h   4. f   5. i   6. b   7. d   8. j   9. c   10. a

Give yourself 1 point for every correct answer: _____

WHAT'S MY SCORE?

TOTAL CORRECT: _____

TOTAL POSSIBLE: ____316____

Chapter Four

A Lot Going On

XVI. NEED SOME ACTION?

Q1. Verbs are well-suited to create clever expressions. Go and insert the right one:

1. He's going to _____ over a new leaf.	a.	play
2. She likes to _____ off the handle.	b.	throw
3. We always _____ a ball when we get together.	c.	get
4. Now you can _____ your own ticket.	d.	pull
5. Slow down—I have to _____ my breath.	e.	ring
6. He had to _____ in the towel.	f.	turn
7. We don't want to _____ the envelope.	g.	have
8. She doesn't want to _____ a stink.	h.	spill
9. Don't try to _____ a stunt like that again.	i.	catch
10. Why don't you _____ it quits?	j.	write
11. He likes to _____ it like it is.	k.	push
12. She's going to _____ the beans.	l.	raise
13. Sorry—it doesn't _____ a bell.	m.	tell
14. I don't want to _____ second fiddle to anyone.	n.	call
15. They always _____ a kick out of it.	o.	fly

Q2. Only one word goes with these action phrases, but you'll need to unscramble them first:

1. **Saw**	**g, Logs**	a.	BATS
2. Play	_____	b.	RSTNU
3. Go	_____	c.	EXDII
4. Make	_____	d.	CREDIASTKDE
5. Tell	_____	e.	RADEBVOOR
6. Keep	_____	f.	ETSI
7. Get	_____	g.	GLOS
8. Take	_____	h.	NESFIRD
9. Cut	_____	i.	BSFI
10. Whistle	_____	j.	OHKYO

Q3.　The verb *to get* is found throughout the English language:

1. I've gotten a lot of _____ out of this old mower.	a.	sack
2. Did you get a _____ of her perfume?	b.	nerve
3. He needs to get back on his _____ again.	c.	heart
4. Can't you get it through your thick _____?	d.	hand
5. She always tries to get in the last _____.	e.	thoughts
6. I need to get up the _____ to ask her.	f.	whiff
7. He worked there until he got the _____.	g.	skull
8. I'm starting to get second _____ about him.	h.	feet
9. I refuse to let him get the upper _____.	i.	mileage
10. We finally got to the _____ of the problem.	j.	word

Q4.　Which verb is missing? Find the one that fits BEST:

1. It all _____ down to one thing.	a.	drew
2. He _____ a beeline for home.	b.	changed
3. I _____ a blank.	c.	bored
4. She _____ a hard bargain.	d.	did
5. It _____ me to tears.	e.	stood
6. We _____ a few corners.	f.	boiled
7. You _____ your tune.	g.	crossed
8. I think that _____ the trick.	h.	made
9. It _____ my mind a few times.	i.	drove
10. They _____ up for their beliefs.	j.	cut

Answers

Q1.　1. f　2. o　3. g　4. j　5. i　6. b　7. k　8. l　9. d　10. n
　　11. m　12. h　13. e　14. a　15. c

Q2.　2. j, hooky　3. e, overboard　4. h, friends　5. i, fibs　6. a, tabs
　　7. d, sidetracked　8. b, turns　9. f, ties　10. c, Dixie

Q3.　1. i　2. f　3. h　4. g　5. j　6. b　7. a　8. e　9. d　10. c

Q4.　1. f　2. h　3. a　4. i　5. c　6. j　7. b　8. d　9. g　10. e

Give yourself 1 point for every correct answer: _____

A LITTLE HISTORY

- At traditional American parties in the eighteenth century, a small ball was often thrown as partners danced around in pairs. In some cases, the dancers had to catch the ball as they sang. Although "balls" are no longer thrown today, the word still means **dance**, while the expression **having a ball** indicates that you are having a good time.
- **To get the sack** used to be **to get the bag**, and it referred to the roving workmen in America who once carried their tools from job to job in a duffel bag. As their job ended, they'd be let go, so over time **getting the sack** became synonymous with being fired and forced to seek employment elsewhere.

BORN IN THE U.S.A.

- Americans can't live without uttering the little word, **get**:

    *My wife **got all worked up** because I didn't **get around** to cleaning the garage today. She wanted **to get a jump** on spring cleaning by **getting rid of** all our extra junk. I guess I'll never **get the hang** of doing chores.*

ON YOUR OWN

1. *Do you know people who **have gotten hitched**?*
2. *What happens when you **get your dander up**?*
3. *When would you say, **Don't get smart with me**?*

Spill the beans

Q5. Can you guess which word belongs in both sentences?

a.	makes	f.	comes
b.	takes	g.	keeps
c.	brings	h.	gives
d.	runs	i.	goes
e.	puts	j.	calls

1. He always _____ up the tab. It _____ in his family.
2. If worst _____ to worst. I hope she _____ to her senses.
3. He _____ house better than I do. That dog never _____ still.
4. She _____ the shots. I hope she _____ his bluff.
5. He usually _____ me the runaround. Who _____ a hoot?
6. She never _____ back on her word. She _____ to bat for us.
7. That _____ me sick. He _____ it from scratch.
8. She _____ things in stride. It _____ one to know one.
9. Let's see if he _____ two and two together. He _____ on airs.
10. She _____ out the worst in me. He _____ home the bacon.

Q6. Select the BEST action words to complete these sentences from the set of scrambled ones on the right: You'll have to…

1. … _____ the line somewhere.   a. OG
2. … _____ the music.   b. UMRD
3. … _____ up some new business.   c. ECMO
4. … _____ up on your Spanish.   d. DHLO
5. … _____ up your act.   e. WARD
6. … _____ the distance.   f. LCLA
7. … _____ to grips with the truth.   g. IGVE
8. … _____ up your end of the bargain.   h. CAFE
9. … _____ off the party.   i. ANCLE
10. … _____ credit where credit is due. j. SBUHR

Q7. Finish up these active one-liners:

1. What goes around …
2. Easy come …
3. If you give them an inch …
4. I'm damned if I do …
5. If I've told you once …

Q8. And what's going on here?

1. She's _____ on the Ritz.	a. turning
2. The car is _____ up again.	b. singing
3. He's _____ low.	c. calling
4. I'm _____ it a shot.	d. running
5. I like _____ my hands dirty.	e. passing
6. We keep _____ into one another.	f. putting
7. They're _____ the plate.	g. getting
8. That's _____ a spade a spade.	h. acting
9. She's _____ the blues.	i. giving
10. He's probably _____ in his grave.	j. laying

Q9. Fill in the right word from the bunch at right.

1. Don't _____ it another thought.	STOP	SLEEP
2. That'll just _____ fuel to the fire.	LEAVE	GO
3. Let's _____ to the chase.	SEE	FIRE
4. We bit off more than we could _____.	PLAY	CHEW
5. I'm beginning to _____ the light.	EAT	HOLD
6. He couldn't _____ less.	SAY	WORK
7. Don't let it _____ to your head.	LIGHT	CUT
8. She will _____ her just desserts.	GET	GIVE
9. It'll eventually _____ to a standstill.	ADD	CARE
10. I'm not going to _____ my breath.	COME	RUN

Answers

Q5. 1. d   2. f   3. g   4. j   5. h   6. i   7. a   8. b   9. e   10. c

Q6. 1. e (draw)   2. h (face)   3. b (drum)   4. j (brush)   5. i (clean)
6. a (go)   7. c (come)   8. d (hold)   9. f (call)   10. g (give)

Q7. 1. comes around   2. easy go   3. they'll take a mile
4. and damned if I don't   5. I've told you a thousand times

Q8. 1. f   2. h   3. j   4. i   5. g   6. d   7. e   8. c   9. b   10. a

Q9. 1. give   2. add   3. cut   4. chew   5. see   6. care   7. go
8. get   9. come   10. hold

Give yourself 1 point for every correct answer:

A LITTLE HISTORY

- The word **ritzy** which means luxurious or elegant, comes from Cesar Ritz, who took over the Hotel Savoy in London in 1892 and later the Ritz-Carlton in New York. It wasn't long before everyone was **putting on the Ritz** as they dressed up to spend a night on the town. Ritz's emphasis on lavishness in service also led to the phrase, **The customer is always right**.

- Throughout the 1800s, anyone who **had the blues** was suffering from alcoholism and the DTs (delirium tremens). Symptoms included sadness, headaches, and visions of pink elephants or **blue devils**. However, as the years passed, people began to equate **the blues** with any form of sadness or depression.

BORN IN THE U.S.A.

- Early America was built on social contact between people who were *coming* from all over the world, and that's why some believe that this word is so common in our vocabulary:

    It'll come as no surprise that it won't come apart at the seams; instead, it'll all come out in the wash and be a dream come true, come hell or high water.

- Folks also use this word as a popular command:

    Come to the point!   Come off it!   Come back!

SAY IT RIGHT

- Simple catch phrases in English put things into action:

    Nature calls and money talks, but crime doesn't pay!

- You can get a lot of mileage out of this word, too:

    Run along, but **don't run down the house;** and if you **run into your friends,** you can **run around with them,** but don't **run up your tab,** or **run off too much at the mouth.**

ON YOUR OWN

1. *Have you ever* **bawled someone out, buckled down**, *or* **butted in?**
2. *Explain how* **tying the knot** *is different from* **settling down**.
3. *When was the last time you* **couldn't take a joke** *or* **couldn't take a hint?**

WORDS OF WISDOM

"Three-fourths of the people you will ever meet are hungering and thirsting for sympathy. Give it to them and they will love you."

Dale Carnegie

XVII. ACTING STRANGE!

Q10. Some verbs are unique or unusual in use and in meaning, offering a great challenge to most. Come on, test yourself:

1. It boggles the _____.
2. She's going to flip her _____.
3. That really piqued my _____.
4. Let's nip it in the _____.
5. Let's not ruffle his _____.

Dirty old man

Q11. With these, find the word with the CLOSEST definition:

1. Snoop around	a.	tamper
2. Blast off	b.	focus
3. Clam up	c.	study
4. Egg on	d.	resolve
5. Drop by	e.	collapse
6. Keel over	f.	decorate
7. Zero in	g.	rescue
8. Iron out	h.	decline
9. Pile up	i.	sneak
10. Mess around	j.	taunt
11. Jazz up	k.	visit
12. Peter out	l.	kiss
13. Bail out	m.	launch
14. Bone up	n.	stack
15. Pucker up	o.	quiet

Q12. Continue to select the BEST word:

1. I was stopped by the cops, and I got …	a.	drafted
2. I went shopping overseas, and I got …	b.	soused
3. I enlisted, and then I got …	c.	dumped
4. I was late for work, and I got …	d.	stuffed
5. I was in a bad relationship, and I got …	e.	booted
6. I was involved in a fight, and I got …	f.	sideswiped
7. I was in a rainstorm, and I got …	g.	gypped
8. I ate a big lunch, and I got …	h.	hooked
9. I joined a secret club, and I got …	i.	frisked
10. I drank at the party, and I got …	j.	decked
11. I was in a wreck, and I got …	k.	blackballed
12. I smoked one cigarette, and I got …	l.	soaked

Answers

Q10. 1. mind   2. lid   3. interest   4. bud   5. feathers
Q11. 1. i   2. m   3. o   4. j   5. k   6. e   7. b   8. d   9. n   10. a
      11. f   12. h   13. g   14. c   15. l

Q12. 1. i   2. g   3. a   4. e   5. c   6. j   7. l   8. d   9. k   10. b
        11. f   12. h

Give yourself 1 point for every correct answer:

A LITTLE HISTORY

- Years ago, appropriate behavior in American society meant that adults had to control their temper in public. A person out of control was compared to a teakettle that **flips its lid** when there's too much heat or pressure. Nowadays, we use the phrase to mean that a person is venting his anger.
- During the 1900s, saltpeter (potassium nitrate) was often used with explosives to mine for gold. When a vein could no longer produce, the miners would say that it simply **petered out**. Today we use the expression to mean that someone or something has died out or gradually come to an end.
- In Creole French, an American dandy was called a *chaste-beaux* (pronounced jazz-bo), who generally stood out because of his fancy mannerisms and clothes. Sometimes, these men competed in cakewalks, where they tried to win the hearts of local women by **jazzing up** their strut or dance steps. Coincidently, the music that was played at these competitions became known as **jazz**.

BORN IN THE U.S.A.

- Americans are masters at adding *on*, *in*, *at*, *out*, and *up* to perfectly innocent verbs and coming out with totally new expressions.

  *Grandma **dolled me up** and **tucked me in**, but never **chewed me out**!*

  *I don't know all the answers, but it just **dawned on me**— we'd both breathe a whole lot easier if we **hashed this thing out**.*

  *There's got to be a better way to **whoop it up** without going totally ape.*

ON YOUR OWN

1. *Do you sashay sometimes?*
2. *Are you capable of ad-libbing?*
3. *Anybody mooching off you?*

Q13. Some activities only involve body parts. Choose the BEST one:

1. hunch your _____	chest	nose	
2. suck your _____	knee	stomach	
3. shake your _____	gums	nails	
4. feast your _____	heart	lip	
5. pick your _____	ankle	feet	
6. snap your _____	elbow	shoulders	
7. polish your _____	toes	neck	
8. steal your _____	bottom	hair	
9. stomp your _____	legs	cheek	
10. button your _____	fingers	throat	
11. spank your _____	chin	hand	
12. braid your _____	thumb	eyes	

Q14. Match more words with similar meanings:

1. bawl	a. gripe
2. tangle	b. hoodwink
3. tattle	c. hoot
4. smooch	d. pawn
5. limp	e. gulp
6. hock	f. swagger
7. howl	g. blubber
8. bellyache	h. thump
9. swig	i. hobble
10. bamboozle	j. kiss
11. wallop	k. blab
12. strut	l. snarl

Hooked on something

Q15. You know what to do here:

1. I'm going to _____ this number down.   a. twiddle
2. They always _____ down the street.   b. guzzle
3. We'll _____ something up for dinner.   c. tip
4. They'll eventually _____ the suspect.   d. swipe
5. I hate to _____ with you.   e. poke
6. Why do you always _____ your sodas?   f. jot
7. All you do is _____ your thumbs.   g. tag
8. Are you going to _____ him off?   h. nab
9. My brother wants to _____ along.   i. root
10. Did you _____ this from the store?   j. whip
11. It's not nice to _____ fun at others.   k. stroll
12. We like to _____ for the home team.   l. bicker

Answers

Q13. 1. shoulders 2. thumb 3. hand 4. eyes 5. nose 6. fingers
      7. nails 8. heart 9. feet 10. lip 11. bottom 12. hair
Q14. 1. g 2. l 3. k 4. j 5. i 6. d 7. c 8. a 9. e 10. b
      11. h 12. f
Q15. 1. f 2. k 3. j 4. h 5. l 6. b 7. a 8. c 9. g 10. d
      11. e 12. i

Give yourself 1 point for every correct answer: _____

A LITTLE HISTORY

- Sir John Wallop led major reprisal raids on the French coast of Normandy in the 1500s against Henry VIII. His easy victories became known as **wallops**, which is why the word today refers to any thorough beating.
- **Jot** refers to the Greek letter *iota*, which was often written merely as a dot below a long vowel. When it was written that way, it was considered the smallest letter in the Greek alphabet. Over the years, any simple process of writing became known as **jotting**, which is how we create handwritten messages today.

- Before zippers were invented, the primary means of closing clothing was with a button. As a result, it wasn't long before Americans began to use the expression **Button your lip** to keep a secret.

BORN IN THE U.S.A.

- Traditional activities in America include *brown-bagging*, *window shopping*, and *thumbing a ride*. Notice how many verbs are graphic descriptions of the action itself. *Horseback riding*, *troubleshooting*, and *hairstyling* are a few more examples.
- Don't forget that English words often have more than one meaning:

   > *You're pathetic! You threw the newspaper **off your lap**, **ran a lap** around the block, and now you want to **lap up** a giant chocolate shake!*

WORDS OF WISDOM

"Only those who dare to fail greatly can ever achieve greatly."
Robert Kennedy

ON YOUR OWN

1. *You can't walk **and do what** at the same time?*
2. *When would you say, **Monkey see, monkey do?***
3. *Are you any good at doing **back flips**, **cartwheels**, or **belly flops?***

XVIII. VICIOUS VERBS!

Q16. All-American English can be pretty violent. This section deals with verbs that sound pretty tough, but in reality are quite tame.

1. That job was _____ on my feet!	a. dead
2. You'll be the _____ of me yet.	b. bloody
3. The band tried to _____ us out.	c. away
4. She was screaming _____ murder.	d. tickled
5. Over my _____ body.	e. time
6. They're getting _____ with murder.	f. kill
7. Till death do us _____.	g. death
8. Let's try to _____ them with kindness.	h. murder
9. I'd be _____ to death if you said yes.	i. drown
10. We've got plenty of _____ to kill.	j. part

Q17. Link each action with the BEST word possible:

1. Shoot	a. the bullet
2. Bury	b. the gun
3. Rock	c. the clock
4. Break	d. the traffic
5. Bite	e. the boat
6. Cut	f. the hatchet
7. Jump	g. the panic button
8. Fight	h. the breeze
9. Punch	i. the mustard
10. Push	j. the news

Q18. And who's responsible? Connect each action with the guilty party:

1. Pushes me around	a. A pitcher
2. Cracks me up	b. A thief
3. Hauls me away	c. A clown
4. Rips me off	d. A bully
5. Strikes me out	e. A policeman

Q19. These demand the same word twice, but fix the answers first:

1. He _____ me for a loop and then _____ me out!
2. He _____ me off and then _____ me down to size!
3. He _____ around the bush and _____ me to the punch!
4. He _____ me blind and then _____ Peter to pay Paul.
5. He _____ a funny joke and then _____ a big smile!
6. He _____ the books and then _____ pay dirt!
7. He _____ his chance and then _____ off some steam!
8. He _____ the habit and then _____ the silence!
9. He _____ out of class and then _____ me off at home.
10. He _____ me the wrong way and then _____ it in.

a. BERBUD
b. DBOREB
c. EROKB
d. ITH
e. TUC
f. PEDPRO
g. DECCARK
h. WEHRT
i. ELWB
j. ABTE

Q20. With these, simply find the BEST match:

1. Racking my brain involves
2. Bursting my bubble involves
3. Twisting my arm involves
4. Busting my gut involves
5. Stealing my heart involves

a. persuasion
b. laughter
c. affection
d. concentration
e. disappointment

Answers

Q16. 1. h   2. g   3. i   4. b   5. a
      6. c   7. j   8. f   9. d   10. e
Q17. 1. h   2. f   3. e   4. j   5. a
      6. i   7. b   8. d   9. c   10. g
Q18. 1. d   2. c   3. e   4. b   5. a
Q19. 1. h (threw)   2. e (cut)
      3. j (beat)   4. b (robbed)
      5. g (cracked)   6. d (hit)
      7. i (blew)   8. c (broke)
      9. f (dropped)   10. a (rubbed)
Q20. 1. d   2. e   3. a   4. b   5. c

Give yourself 1 point for every correct answer: _____

Dime a dozen

A LITTLE HISTORY

- For Native Americans, the hatchet carried the same symbolic significance as did the sword for the European settlers. In order to secure a treaty with a warring tribe, a colonial representative had to attend a ceremony where the local chief would literally **bury the hatchet** as a sign of peace. In modern times, the expression suggests that one is willing to end a dispute and stop the fighting for good.

- Both **rock the boat** and **make waves** are nautical expressions that mean that someone is upsetting calm waters, and making life difficult for everyone else on board. Nowadays, **Don't rock the boat!** commands a person to refrain from doing anything that might upset a stable situation.

- Using lights and sticks, fifteenth century nocturnal hunters used the technique of **beating around the bush** in an effort to stir birds out of their nests. They had to be clever and careful, which is why the phrase describes a cautious, evasive person who refuses to come to the point.

- **Thrown for a loop** is an aeronautical expression that refers to being suddenly knocked out of a flight pattern and forced to use a looping maneuver in order to recover. Today, it means to disorient someone by doing something totally unexpected.

BORN IN THE U.S.A.

- Talk about a creative language! When a person dies in the U.S., they don't just **pass away**. We also say that they *bit the dust, bought the farm, gave up the ghost, went to meet their Maker, cashed in their chips, kicked the bucket*, and started *pushing up daisies*!

ON YOUR OWN

1. Do you usually *roll with the punches when push comes to shove*?
2. More ways than you *can shake a what*?
3. How would you use the word *smithereens*?
4. Ever *locked horns* with someone?

Q21. The missing words below are spelled backwards here:

1. Let's _____ a bite to eat.
2. I really get a _____ out of her stories.
3. Can you _____ this twenty?
4. He likes to _____ off his mouth.
5. That's a real _____ act to follow.
6. It'll just add _____ to injury.
7. They gave him the old _____.
8. I'll never get the _____ of it!
9. This cash will _____ a hole in my pocket.
10. You couldn't _____ the broad side of a barn.

a. TLUSNI
b. TOOHS
c. HGUOT
d. TIH
e. GNAH
f. NRUB
g. BARG
h. KCIK
i. KAERB
j. OHEVAEH

Q22. These brutal acts are in the past tense. Find the BEST one:

1. The clock _____ one.
2. My ears just _____.
3. The boss _____ down all my ideas.
4. They _____ us to the punch.
5. I _____ around the house all day.
6. They _____ the problem head-on.
7. The supermarket _____ their prices.
8. Our kids _____ tooth and nail.
9. He _____ the habit.
10. That really _____ my socks off.

a. tackled
b. slashed
c. hung
d. knocked
e. fought
f. popped
g. beat
h. struck
i. shot
j. kicked

Q23. Connect:

1. to needle = _____
2. to mug = _____
3. to brain = _____
4. to bust = _____
5. to frame = _____
6. to jinx = _____
7. to snitch = _____
8. to wrestle = _____
9. to boot = _____
10. to croak = _____

a. to can
b. to rat
c. to bug
d. to expire
e. to grapple
f. to bean
g. to pinch
h. to curse
i. to batter
j. to trap

Q24. Now fill in the blanks. One answer is hidden in each string of letters:

1. He took a _____ at it.
2. You need a _____ course in table manners.
3. She told me to _____ by later.
4. You'll find it _____ ahead.
5. That really _____ the spot.
6. We have to _____ out violence on T.V.
7. I was so mad, I wanted to _____ his neck.
8. As an actor, I always _____ my lines.
9. That shirt is going to _____ with your sweater.
10. She's a nervous _____ during tax time.

a. CAWRINGSIDEDO
b. ABUTCHERRYTO
c. CLASHINGFORTS
d. EWRECKINGANG
e. FLOODROPOSSE
f. ESTABLEASHESS
g. SUCRASHEDIED
h. KILLEDEADEED
i. STAMPERINGUTS
j. CHITCHATTINGO

Answers

Q21. 1. g, grab   2. h, kick   3. i, break   4. b, shoot   5. c, tough
6. a, insult   7. j, heaveho   8. e, hang   9. f, burn   10. d, hit
Q22. 1. h   2. f   3. i   4. g   5. c   6. a   7. b   8. e   9. j   10. d
Q23. 1. c   2. i   3. f   4. g   5. j   6. h   7. b   8. e   9. a   10. d
Q24. 1. f, stab   2. g, crash   3. e, drop   4. h, dead   5. j, hit   6. i, stamp
7. a, wring   8. b, butcher   9. c, clash   10. d, wreck

Give yourself 1 point for every correct answer:

A LITTLE HISTORY

- **To get a kick** or a **charge** or a **bang** out of something comes from the early twentieth century, when Americans began to depend upon mechanical devices in everyday life. Electrical machines, for example, often jolted their owners, while gas-powered automobiles would jump as they backfired. Such sudden exhilaration made life exciting, which is why these expressions relate to thrills and enjoyment today.

- **To needle**, which means **to bother or pester** someone, comes from the old tailor's joke of pricking a coworker with a needle in order to lighten the mood. Working as a tailor or seamstress was a grueling job before it became an industry, and workers often sought a little levity to get through their difficult workday.

Dog tag

- **To add insult to injury** comes from the Aesop fable about the bald-headed man who tries to kill a fly on his plate. In doing so, he ends up injuring himself. The fly asks, **What will you do to yourself, since you have added insult to injury?** The phrase still means to heap scorn on someone who is already hurt.

BORN IN THE U.S.A.

- Throughout the U.S., Americans make violent references to just about anything:

  *He may **blow a gasket**, **blow the whistle** on someone, and then **blow town**, or **throw a party**, **throw a tantrum**, and then **throw in the towel**; on the other hand, he might **hit the jackpot**, **hit the sauce**, and then **hit a person below the belt!***

SAY IT RIGHT

- All-American English also uses compound forms to express ***rough-and-tumble*** action:

  At work, for example, some folks like **to backstab**, while their bosses are putting employees **through the meat grinder**. At home, some kids like **to roughhouse**, while their parents go on the **warpath**. Meanwhile, life goes on **at breakneck speed**…

? ON YOUR OWN

1. *This is just a **shot in the dark**, but have you ever been in a **knock-down-drag-out fight** at a **no-holds-barred** affair?*
2. *Have you ever met a **dead ringer** for a movie star?*
3. *When was the last time you saw a **shooting gallery**?*
4. *Name someone who's a **goner**.*

WORDS OF WISDOM

"Nothing in the world is more dangerous than sincere ignorance and conscientious stupidity."

Dr. Martin Luther King, Jr.

XIX. PLAYING AROUND!

Q25. Now that all that rough stuff is behind us, let's turn toward a lighter side: the world of sports and recreation.

1. This job is just child's _____.	a. shot
2. He's definitely met his _____.	b. ball
3. I'm not sure at this stage in the _____.	c. player
4. That's par for the _____.	d. play
5. She's nothing but a spoil- _____.	e. game
6. Once the music started, we all had a _____.	f. sport
7. I told you it wasn't in the _____.	g. field
8. She's a real team _____.	h. cards
9. Don't take chances on a long _____.	i. course
10. We've got to level the playing _____.	j. match

Q26. Hey, sports fans—can you put all these words together correctly?

1. **slam**	a. ball
2. off	b. down
3. shot	c. stick
4. prize	d. run
5. foul	e. slam
6. fore	f. put
7. home	g. iron
8. touch	h. chip
9. pole	i. **dunk**
10. grand	j. time
11. penalty	k. sides
12. nine	l. vault
13. poker	m. fight
14. cue	n. box
15. over	o. hand

Q27. Many famous expressions come from baseball. Find the right words:

1. Thanks for going to _____ for me.	glove	base
2. They want to play hard _____ with us.	umpire	park
3. Sorry, but you're way off _____.	double	strike
4. I know you like her, but you're batting _____.	leagues	tag
5. We became friends _____ off the bat.	eye	bunt
6. That price was in the general ball_____.	swing	bat
7. Remember to keep your _____ on the ball.	game	inning
8. Take me out to the ball_____.	runs	zero
9. You're in the big _____ now.	cap	right
10. I don't want to _____ out on our first date.	field	ball

Answers

Q25 1. d   2. j   3. e   4. i   5. f   6. b   7. h   8. c   9. a   10. g

Q26. 2. k   3. f   4. m   5. a   6. o   7. d   8. b   9. l   10. e   11. n
  12. g   13. h   14. c   15. j

Q27. 1. bat   2. ball   3. base   4. zero   5. right   6. park   7. eye
  8. game   9. leagues   10. strike

Give yourself 1 point for every correct answer: _____

BORN IN THE U.S.A.

- The world of sports in the United States ranges from winter to water to extreme. Have you ever noticed how often Americans refer to card games?

    I put all my cards on the table, so ante up. If you play your cards right, you'll have a winning hand and take home everything in the kitty.

SAY IT RIGHT

- Hundreds of verbs in English are linked to the realm of sport:

    I sit here in the stands and heckle and cheer, while they're out there trying to pass, catch, shoot, hit, block, dribble, and score!

A LITTLE HISTORY

- It was quite a challenge for early American gunners to fire their cannons with accuracy at great distances, so most aimed at relatively close targets. A longer shot was much too difficult and was seldom attempted. The expression **long shot** has changed in meaning, but still suggests an attempt at something that probably won't succeed.
- The **home run** originated in the mid-nineteenth century to designate a hit that allows a batter in baseball to round all the bases, reach **home** plate, and score a run. The first major league **home run king** was Babe Ruth, who hit 60 homers in 1927.
- **Answering the bell** alludes to a boxing match in which a bell is sounded to signal the beginning of the next round. If a boxer is too hurt to return, the other one wins, because his opponent is not able **to answer the bell** and continue the fight. The expression has acquired a broader meaning, that is, to meet any imposed demands or respond to a specific challenge.

ON YOUR OWN

1. *Do you like to watch **NASCAR**, **WWF**, or the **PGA** on TV?*
2. *What's the difference between a **hook shot** and a **slap shot**?*
3. *How many **leg lifts**, **jumping jacks**, and **push ups** can you do?*

WORDS OF WISDOM

"Baseball is 90% mental, the other half is physical."

Yogi Berra

Q28. Which sports do these words probably refer to?

1. field goal _____
2. red card _____
3. side pocket _____
4. free throw _____
5. line drive _____
6. high jump _____
7. chip shot _____
8. blue line _____
9. first serve _____
10. left jab _____

Q29. Keep going—name the sport:

1. You're outta there! _____
2. Fore! _____
3. Hike! _____
4. Goal! _____
5. Jump ball! _____

Drink like a fish

Q30. Stay with the pattern. What sports are featured at these popular events?

1. World Series   _____
2. Final Four   _____
3. Stanley Cup   _____
4. Wimbledon   _____
5. Kentucky Derby   _____
6. World Cup   _____
7. Super Bowl   _____
8. Indianapolis 500   _____
9. The Masters   _____

Answers

Q28.   1. football   2. soccer   3. pool   4. basketball   5. baseball
      6. track & field   7. golf   8. hockey   9. tennis   10. boxing

Q29.   1. baseball   2. golf   3. football   4. soccer   5. basketball

Q30.   1. baseball   2. basketball   3. hockey   4. tennis
      5. horse racing   6. soccer   7. football   8. auto racing   9. golf

Give yourself 1 point for every correct answer: _____

BORN IN THE U.S.A.

- Americans continue to build rinks, tracks, courts, diamonds, fields, parks, stadiums, and arenas in cities everywhere due to their incredible passion for sports. Sociologists believe this is why folks from the U.S. are often more direct and competitive in business.

SAY IT RIGHT

- The word **sport** can be used in a variety of ways:

  The sportsman in the sports shirt has a sporty new sports car.

- In our country, it's always important to use words related to sports correctly. In tennis, for example, you try to win the **match**, instead of just a **game**. Moreover, the NBA **Finals** is never called a **tourney.** And the **title** fight? I'm talking boxing, of course!

ON YOUR OWN

1. *What do you like about the **7th inning stretch**?*
2. *Are you familiar with the **Tar Heels**, the **Crimson Tide**, or the **Buckeyes**?*
3. *Have you ever shot a **bogey**, **birdie**, or **eagle**?*

A LITTLE HISTORY

• American James A. Naismith invented **basketball** in 1891, when he was asked to develop a team sport that could be played indoors during the winter. The first **baskets** were actually **peach baskets**, and everyone played with the same ball that was used for soccer.

XX. KID'S STUFF!

Q31. Kids are the real experts at play, so when it comes to fun and make-believe, we must listen carefully to what they have to say. Have you ever played . . .

1. Tiddly_____? W _____
2. Pin-the-tail-on-the-_____? D _____
3. Tug-a-_____? W _____
4. Follow the_____? L _____
5. _____-scotch? H _____
6. _____ Says? S _____
7. _____ and Seek? H _____
8. Blind Man's _____? B _____
9. _____ the Flag? C _____
10. Dodge _____? B _____
11. _____ Frog? L _____
12. Musical _____? C _____

Q32. Now create some all-American playthings:

1. stuffed	a. board
2. board	b. figures
3. roller	c. hoop
4. skate	d. blocks
5. modeling	e. rope
6. action	f. airplanes
7. train	g. book
8. hula	h. animals
9. jump	i. games
10. coloring	j. clay
11. building	k. set
12. model	l. blades

Q33. These names sound familiar to most children:

1. Teddy _____	a. Box
2. _____ Joe	b. Doll
3. Jack-in-the-_____	c. Raggedy
4. Barbie _____	d. G.I.
5. _____ Anne	e. Bear

Q34. Keep going:

1. _____ Potato Head	a. Doctor
2. _____ Fairy Tales	b. Aesop's
3. _____ Goose	c. Mister
4. _____ Fables	d. Mother
5. _____ Seuss	e. Grimm's

Fall off the wagon

Q35. What are the kids doing? Careful—the answers are spelled
       backwards:

1.	Reading	a.	SETIK
2.	Running	b.	OEDIV SEMAG
3.	Going	c.	DUM SEIP
4.	Taking	d.	SKCANS
5.	Skipping	e.	YTTOP
6.	Flying	f.	SKOOBYROTS
7.	Watching	g.	SYALER
8.	Playing	h.	SPAN
9.	Making	i.	SENOTS
10.	Munching	j.	SNOOTRAC

Q36. Years ago, these were in the kid's room:

1.	Tinker	a.	horse
2.	Trading	b.	skates
3.	Sling	c.	men
4.	Rocking	d.	toys
5.	Pop	e.	set
6.	Lincoln	f.	cards
7.	Roller	g.	gun
8.	Dart	h.	logs
9.	Army	i.	shot
10.	Tea	j.	board

Answers

Q31. 1. winks   2. donkey   3. war   4. leader   5. hop   6. Simon
      7. Hide   8. Bluff   9. Capture   10. Ball   11. Leap   12. Chairs

Q32. 1. h   2. i   3. l   4. a   5. j   6. b   7. k   8. c   9. e   10. g
      11. d   12. f

Q33. 1. e   2. d   3. a   4. b   5. c

Q34. 1. c   2. e   3. d   4. b   5. a

Q35. 1. f   2. g   3. e   4. h   5. i   6. a   7. j   8. b   9. c   10. d

Q36. 1. d   2. f   3. i   4. a   5. g   6. h   7. b   8. j   9. c   10. e

Give yourself 1 point for every correct answer:

ALL AMERICAN CROSSWORD 4

Across

1. Miles _____ hour.
5. I had to drown my _____.
6. Actions speak _____ than words.
7. ____ Mice and Men.
10. I was _____ man out.
11. Like a bridge over _____ waters.
12. It went to and ____.
14. It's about _____.
15. (means jail, hoosegow)
16. ____ help me God.

Down

1. I was _____ as a peacock.
2. One _____ the money…
3. It was ____ drawer.
4. _____ and you shall receive.
5. It's my _____ blanket.
8. We read Aesop's _____.
9. You should _____ your mind.
10. They did it ____ the cuff.
13. I went to the ____ Grande.

A finished crossword is on page 242.

A LITTLE HISTORY

- In 1902, when President Theodore Roosevelt was on a hunting expedition in Mississippi, his party caught a black bear and tied it to a tree. When the president arrived, he felt pity for the lean, exhausted animal, and stated that to shoot it would not be sportsmanlike. After the story hit the newsstands, a novelty store made up some stuffed toy animals and called them **Teddy bears**. Americans have been buying them ever since.

BORN IN THE U.S.A.

- *Before Transformers, Lego, and Game Boy, most American kids spent time outdoors on **teeter-totters**, **jungle gyms**, **swing sets**, and **merry-go-rounds**. Many went exploring or fishing, while others built forts or tree houses. Concerns about safety changed all that, and the majority of kids today play indoor games using the T.V. or computer.*

ON YOUR OWN

1. *Did you ever own a **Radio Flyer?** An **Etch-a-sketch? Play-doh?***
2. *Fill in the blanks if you know anything about toys:*

   My _____ Pony

   Cabbage _____ Kids

   Teenage _____ Turtles

   _____ Rangers

   Beanie _____

3. *What comes to mind with **Lionel? Crayola? Matchbox? Schwinn? Marvel?***
4. *Have you ever made **sling shots, spit wads,** or **pea shooters?***
5. *What is the moral of **The Hare and the Tortoise?** How about **The Little Engine that Could?***

WORDS OF WISDOM

"Do not let what you cannot do interfere with what you can do."

John Wooden

Q37. Children across the U.S. learn to sing all of the words below:

1. Ring-around-the-_____, ...
2. London _____ is falling down, ...
3. The farmer in the _____, ...
4. _____-a-bye, baby, ...
5. Skip to the _____, ...
6. _____ goes the weasel, ...
7. Old MacDonald had a _____, ...
8. Over the river and through the _____, ...
9. Who's afraid of the big, bad _____, ...
10. I'm a little tea _____, ...

Q38. Do you know these rhymes? Unscramble the letters first:

BTU   LHIL   RENROC   NSO
TAERE   LALW   OLSU
LEDFID   TAKBSE   PEHES

1. Peter, Peter, Pumpkin _____
2. Little Bo Peep has lost her _____
3. Tom, Tom, the Piper's _____
4. Old King Cole was a merry old _____
5. Jack and Jill went up the _____
6. A tisket, a tasket, a green and yellow _____
7. Little Jack Horner sat in a _____
8. Hey, diddle, diddle, the cat and the _____
9. Humpty Dumpty sat on a _____
10. Rub-a-dub-dub, three men in a _____

Q39. Stay in the land of make-believe, and finish these famous one-liners:

1. The boy who cried _____.
2. There was an old woman who lived in a _____.
3. Little Red Riding _____.
4. Little Boy Blue, come blow your _____.
5. Mary had a little _____.
6. Sing a song of _____.
7. Jack and the _____.
8. Three blind _____.
9. Little Miss Muffet sat on a _____.
10. Goldilocks and the three _____.

Q40. Listen in on the little ones:

1. I've got _____ on that chocolate!
2. Mind your own _____!
3. Finders keepers, losers _____!
4. Last one there is a rotten _____!
5. Sticks and stones may break my _____!
6. Cross my _____ and hope to die!
7. I double _____ you!
8. Yech—she's got _____!
9. Don't _____ out!
10. Say _____!

a. chicken
b. heart
c. uncle
d. dare
e. dibs
f. cooties
g. weepers
h. bones
i. egg
j. beeswax

Answers

Q37. 1. rosey   2. bridge   3. dell   4. Rock   5. loo   6. Pop
7. farm   8. woods   9. wolf   10. pot

Q38. 1. eater   2. sheep   3. son   4. soul   5. hill   6. basket
7. corner   8. fiddle   9. wall   10. tub

Q39. 1. wolf   2. shoe   3. Hood   4. horn   5. lamb   6. sixpence
7. beanstalk   8. mice   9. tuffet   10. bears

Q40. 1. e   2. j   3. g   4. i   5. h   6. b   7. d   8. f   9. a   10. c

Give yourself 1 point for every correct answer: _____

A LITTLE HISTORY

- According to some historians, centuries ago a Roman found himself in trouble, so he called out to the closest family member for help, **patrue mi patruissime**, which means "uncle, my best of uncles." That is why today, children **cry uncle** whenever they are forced to give up, ask for help, or admit defeat.

ON YOUR OWN

1. *Fill in the missing words, and name the story they come from:*

   I'll huff and I'll puff, … _____

   Fee-Fi-Fo-Fum, … _____

   What big eyes you have, … _____

2. *Have you ever read about* **Uncle Remus? Tom Thumb?** **The Pied Piper?**
3. *Say all of this rhyme aloud:* **"Hickory dickory dock, …"**

WORDS OF WISDOM

"You may fool all the people some of the time; you can even fool some of the people all of the time; but you can't fool all of the people all of the time."

Phineas Barnum

WHAT'S MY SCORE?

TOTAL CORRECT: _____

TOTAL POSSIBLE: ___391___

Chapter Five

Mighty Messages

XXI. MOM USED TO SAY!

Q1. Let's start off with a few classic phrases from Mom herself. You should know them by heart:

1. If I've told you once, I've told you a _____ times!
2. All's well that ends _____!
3. Better to be safe than _____!
4. Beauty is in the eye of the _____!
5. _____ doesn't grow on trees!
6. What goes around, _____ around!
7. If the _____ fits, wear it!
8. Never look a gift _____ in the mouth!
9. The early _____ gets the worm!
10. Nothing ventured, nothing _____!
11. Cleanliness is next to _____!
12. Two wrongs don't make a _____!
13. _____ is the best policy!
14. Everything comes to those who _____!
15. Every _____ has a silver lining!
16. A penny saved is a penny _____!
17. Neither a borrower nor a _____ be!
18. One good _____ deserves another!
19. _____ is only skin deep!
20. Beggars can't be _____!

Q2. Has anyone ever told you these before?

1. You can't win them _____.
2. You can't beat a dead _____.
3. You can't please _____.
4. You can't teach an old _____ new tricks.
5. You can't make a silk purse out of a sow's _____.

Q3. Use only the key words to create a complete saying:

1. glass houses   **People in glass houses should not throw stones.**

2. bird in the hand   _____

3. count your chickens   _____

4. burn the candle   _____

5. say anything nice   _____

6. early to bed   _____

7. spilt milk   _____

8. have your cake   _____

9. going gets tough   _____

10. flock together   _____

11. throw the baby   _____

12. you don't succeed   _____

Q4. Find Mom's favorite command. Select the BEST one:

1. _____ your step!   a. forgive
2. _____ your manners!   b. take
3. _____ your lucky stars!   c. count
4. _____ your tongue!   d. grin
5. _____ to your guns!   e. watch
6. _____ sleeping dogs lie! f. stick
7. _____ while the iron is hot! g. waste
8. _____ the bull by the horns! h. let
9. _____ your blessings!   i. hold
10. _____ and forget!   j. thank
11. _____ and bear it!   k. strike
12. _____ not, want not!   l. mind

Answers

Q1. 1. thousand   2. well   3. sorry   4. beholder   5. Money
6. comes   7. shoe   8. horse   9. bird   10. gained
11. Godliness   12. right   13. Honesty   14. wait   15. cloud
16. earned   17. lender   18. turn   19. Beauty   20. choosers

Q2. 1. all   2. horse   3. everyone   4. dog   5. ear

Q3.   2. A bird in the hand is worth two in the bush.

3. Don't count your chickens before they hatch.

4. Don't burn the candle at both ends.

5. If you can't say anything nice, don't say anything at all.

6. Early to bed, early to rise, makes a man healthy, wealthy, and wise.

7. Don't cry over spilt milk.

8. You can't have your cake and eat it, too.

9. When the going gets tough, the tough get going.

10. Birds of a feather flock together.

11. Don't throw out the baby with the bath water.

12. If at first you don't succeed, try, try again.

Q4.   1. e   2. l   3. j   4. i   5. f   6. h   7. k   8. b   9. c   10. a
11. d   12. g

**Give yourself 1 point for every correct answer:**

A LITTLE HISTORY

- When Americans traveled either on horseback or by horse-drawn carriage, the animal would occasionally lie down, especially if it were tired, sick, or elderly. Owners didn't always have patience with their horses, so they'd flog them until they got up and started moving again. However, if the poor animal were dead, they'd end up **flogging a dead horse** for quite a long time. Today, the expression refers to doing something with futility, or belaboring an issue that is no longer of any concern.

- **Grin and abide** was the original command to sailors in the eighteenth century, as they struggled with the rough weather and seas on an extended voyage. It was later changed to **grin and bear it**, but it still means to make the best of a difficult situation today.

ON YOUR OWN

1. *What happened when **curiosity killed the cat**?*
2. *For you, what makes **the heart grow fonder**?*
3. *Do you know of **any animal that doesn't change its spots**?*

WORDS OF WISDOM

"Good fences make good neighbors."

Benjamin Franklin

Q5. Do you need some more advice? Search for the answers here:

1. Don't bite the _____ that feeds you!
2. Don't burn your _____ behind you!
3. Don't cut off your _____ to spite your face!
4. Don't bite off more than you can _____!
5. Don't make a _____ out of a molehill!
6. Don't put all your eggs in one _____!
7. Don't go barking up the wrong _____!
8. Don't toot your own _____!
9. Don't believe everything you _____!
10. Don't judge a book by its _____!

BUSH	HORN
HEAR	NEST
PLATE	TABLES
MOUNTAIN	LEG
NOSE	COOK
TREE	HAND
HOUSE	COVER
CHEW	BRIDGES
PAGES	SEE
STUDY	BASKET

Q6. Finish what you started!

1. Too many cooks …
2. A stitch in time …
3. Don't leave for tomorrow …
4. All that glitters …
5. He who laughs last …
6. Out of sight …
7. The bigger they are …
8. A rolling stone …
9. What a tangled web we weave …
10. A place for everything …
11. All work and no play …
12. While the cat's away …
13. You can lead a horse to water …
14. Where there's a will …
15. What's good for the goose …

Five o'clock shadow

Q7. Take a minute to straighten out some one-liners:

1. thicker is water blood than   **Blood is thicker than water**
2. late than better never   _____
3. is hesitates he lost who   _____
4. each own to his   _____
5. merrier more the the   _____

Q8. Here are more words to the wise:

1. _____ bygones be bygones!	a. Learn
2. _____ credit where credit is due!	b. Live
3. _____ your nose to the grindstone!	c. Sleep
4. _____ from your mistakes!	d. Look
5. _____ at the bright side!	e. Save
6. _____ do with what you have!	f. Let
7. _____ and smell the roses!	g. Make
8. _____ for a rainy day!	h. Stop
9. _____ tight!	i. Give
10. _____ and learn!	j. Keep

Answers

Q5. 1. hand   2. bridges   3. nose   4. chew   5. mountain
    6. basket   7. tree   8. horn   9. hear   10. cover

Q6. 1. spoil the broth   2. saves nine   3. what you can do today
    4. is not gold   5. laughs best   6. out of mind
    7. the harder they fall   8. gathers no moss
    9. when we practice to deceive   10. and everything in its place
    11. makes Jack a dull boy   12. the mice will play
    13. but you can't make it drink   14. there's a way
    15. is good for the gander

Q7. 2. Better late than never.
    3. He who hesitates is lost.
    4. To each his own.
    5. The more the merrier.

Q8. 1. f 2. i 3. j 4. a 5. d 6. g 7. h 8. e 9. c 10. b

Give yourself 1 point for every correct answer:

A LITTLE HISTORY

- The value of a horse is primarily determined by its age, and the age of a horse is determined by looking at its teeth. In nineteenth century America, one of the greatest gifts a person could receive was a horse. However, one would **never look a gift horse in the mouth**, because that would be questioning the value of the gift that was just received.
- The expression, **What's sauce for the goose is sauce for the gander**, originated in the 1600s and it referred to the fact that whatever sauce you used for a cooked **goose** (female of the species) would taste the same if you put it on a cooked **gander** (male of the species). In other words, what's good for one person or situation is equally good for another.

BORN IN THE U.S.A.

- Some American moms have encouraged their children to be independent, and some of their expressions have become classics:

    You need to pull yourself up by your own bootstraps, believe in yourself, and remember this above all—to thine own self be true!

ON YOUR OWN

1. *How do Americans combine **haste** with **waste**?*
2. *And what has **practice** to do with **perfection**?*
3. *What is believed to be **greener on the other side**?*

WORDS OF WISDOM

"We should not only use all the brains we have, but all that we can borrow."

Woodrow Wilson

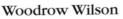

XXII. THE RELIGIOUS PAST!

Q9. All-American English is filled with expressions that heal, encourage, and provide hope…but here the answers are all mixed up:

RTBETI   NWI   HPSI   CUPSHEN   NKSI
OG   PU   ENDO   YDA   ENAPHP   SALNP
MCARE   DLROW   HTOSR   EAKM

1. Don't fret—it's not the end of the _____.
2. Life is too _____ to worry about it.
3. Easy come, easy _____.
4. Let's just try to _____ the most of it.
5. There's more than one way to _____ a cat.
6. Keep your chin _____.
7. Take it one _____ at a time.
8. Even the best laid _____ go awry.
9. Don't give up the _____.
10. What's done is _____.
11. Accidents will _____.
12. You have to take the _____ with the sweet.
13. You _____ some, you lose some.
14. The _____ always rises to the top.
15. You should just roll with the _____.

Rock-a-bye baby

Q10. Don't forget that Americans have always turned to God in times of need. This selection includes some religious vocabulary:

1. That's the _____ truth.
2. To err is human; to _____ divine.
3. We may have to move _____ and earth to do it.
4. I won't tell a single _____.
5. Speaking of the _____.
6. She put her hand on the _____.
7. At dinner, we asked him to say _____.
8. I think you're preaching to the _____.
9. Practice what you _____.
10. They want to have a large _____ wedding.

a. grace
b. Bible
c. church
d. preach
e. choir
f. gospel
g. soul
h. heaven
i. devil
j. forgive

Q11. All of the following include the word **God**:

1. If you get fired, God _____, we'll probably lose the house.
2. I said, "God _____ you," after you sneezed.
3. God only _____ what she does in her spare time.
4. He _____ to God he's innocent.
5. I'm going to finish, so _____ me God.
6. Those farmers are humble, God-_____ people.
7. I bid you God-_____ on your journey.
8. He's in a God-_____ mess with his ex-wife.
9. In God we _____.
10. You are truly a God-_____!
11. They preach the _____ of God at that church.
12. That guy was blessed with some God-_____ talent.
13. One _____, under God.
14. I hate this God-_____ place!
15. For God's _____, would you please be quiet!

a. send
b. help
c. nation
d. awful
e. sake
f. word
g. swears
h. given
i. fearing
j. knows
k. forsaken
l. forbid
m. bless
n. trust
o. speed

Answers

Q9. 1. world 2. short 3. go 4. make 5. skin 6. up 7. day
8. plans 9. ship 10. done 11. happen 12. bitter 13. win
14. cream 15. punches

Q10. 1. f 2. j 3. h 4. g 5. i 6. b 7. a 8. e 9. d 10. c

Q11. 1. l 2. m 3. j 4. g 5. b 6. i 7. o 8. d 9. n 10. a
11. f 12. h 13. c 14. k 15. e

A LITTLE HISTORY

- Our national motto, **In God we trust**, came about due to the strong religious sentiment during the Civil War. The words first appeared on April 22, 1864 on the newly minted two-cent coins, and since then have been printed on every form of U.S. currency.
- In olden times, it was believed that evil things would appear the moment you mentioned the devil's name. Today, we jokingly say **speaking of the devil** whenever somebody who was recently mentioned shows up.

BORN IN THE U.S.A.

- As Americans traveled long distances in colonial times, their expressions underwent changes even when they still referred to the same thing:

    *My **pastor** used the **Good Book** to explain **Glory Land**, while your **preacher** used the **Scriptures** to explain life beyond the **Pearly Gates**.*

ON YOUR OWN

1. *Recite the **Golden Rule**.*
2. *You **praise the Lord and pass the** what?*
3. *Your what **runneth over?***

WORDS OF WISDOM

"It is better to be thought of as a fool, than to open your mouth
and remove all doubt."

The Book of Proverbs

Q12. Most people in the U.S. are exposed to the words below.
They come from the Bible:

1. _____ not, lest ye be judged …
2. Whoever casts the first _____ …
3. The mind is willing, but the flesh is _____ …
4. As you shall sow, so shall you _____…
5. It is better to _____ than to receive …

Q13. Stay with the classic sayings:

1. Man cannot live by _____ alone.
2. Hell hath no fury like a _____ scorned.
3. God helps those who help _____.
4. The road to _____ is paved with good intentions.
5. _____ is the root of all evil.

Q14. People in love say nice things, too.

1. baby	a. heart
2. dream	b. bird
3. lamb	c. dove
4. sugar	d. bunch
5. butter	e. doll
6. turtle	f. throb
7. honey	g. chop
8. sweet	h. boat
9. love	i. plum
10. heart	j. cup

Q15. Continue to create phrases related to romance:

1. It was nothing more than _____ love.   a. tree
2. He went out on a _____ date.   b. blue
3. We used to _____ out on the porch swing.   c. heart
4. She loves me, she loves me _____.   d. music
5. I've got a _____ on you.   e. cupid
6. Will you be my _____?   f. flowers
7. She got bored and gave him the _____.   g. hugs
8. We could make beautiful _____ together.   h. blind
9. I fell _____ over heels in love.   i. make
10. Let's carve our initials in this _____.   j. sweet
11. I love you a bushel and a _____.   k. knot
12. She sends you lots of _____ and kisses!   l. puppy
13. You broke my _____.   m. fair
14. Roses are red, violets are _____.   n. brush-off
15. Whisper _____ nothings in my ear.   o. head
16. You don't bring me _____ any more!   p. crush
17. Is he your _____ in shining armor?   q. valentine
18. All is _____ in love and war.   r. peck
19. She always tries to play _____.   s. knight
20. I think it's time we tied the _____.   t. not

Flea market

Answers

Q12. 1. Judge   2. stone   3. weak   4. reap   5. give
Q13. 1. bread   2. woman   3. themselves   4. hell   5. Money
Q14. 1. e   2. h   3. g   4. i   5. j   6. c   7. d   8. a   9. b   10. f
Q15. 1. l   2. h   3. i   4. t   5. p   6. q   7. n   8. d   9. o   10. a   11. r
       12. g   13. c   14. b   15. j   16. f   17. s   18. m   19. e   20. k

Give yourself 1 point for every correct answer:

A LITTLE HISTORY

- Much like in Japan and in parts of India today, early American customs included the symbolic **tying of the hands** at a wedding ceremony, and the man and woman were not allowed to untie the knot until they consummated the marriage. In modern times, the expression **tying the knot** simply refers to getting married.
- Historically, the word **puppy** comes from the French *poupée*, meaning **doll** or **plaything**. However, the expression **puppy love** probably refers to the innocent, playful, and puppy-like antics of two youngsters who are infatuated with one another.
- **Valentine's Day** is named after St. Valentine, who was martyred in the year 270, and has long been associated with the union of lovers under conditions of duress. It is celebrated on February 14 with the exchanging of greeting cards, which were first produced in the United States in the 1840s.

BORN IN THE U.S.A.

- Love and truly American English have mixed well throughout history:

  *When your grandfather was my **beau**, we used **to neck** by the wishing well near **lover's lane**. He was a **sweet-talking ladies' man**, and I fell for him in a **kissing booth** at the state fair. So, now you know why we had to **elope!***

WORDS OF WISDOM

"The sweetest joy, the wildest woe is love."

Pearl Bailey

? ON YOUR OWN

1. *Do you know the **Lord's Prayer**?*
2. *Where might you hear the words, **Ashes to ashes, dust to dust...**?*
3. *When was the last time you heard, **Dearly beloved, we are gathered...**?*

XXIII. EXPRESS YOURSELF!

Q16. As long as we're being passionate, we might as well start raising our voices:

1. Boy oh _____!	a. goodness
2. For crying out _____!	b. holy
3. How in the _____?	c. grief
4. What on _____?	d. kidding
5. _____ cow!	e. gosh
6. Good _____, Charlie Brown!	f. boy
7. You've got to be _____!	g. me
8. _____ gracious!	h. oh
9. _____ whiz!	i. loud
10. _____ darn it!	j. earth
11. _____ dear!	k. gee
12. Dear _____!	l. world

Q17. Unscramble these letters to form more expressions:

1. KISEY!   _____
2. EPJSERE!   _____
3. WWO!   _____
4. HGSO!   _____
5. GMAUDD!   _____
6. LOYLG!   _____
7. KUSSCH!   _____
8. GNDA!   _____
9. DKOGOSAZ!   _____
10. KCHE!   _____

Q18. Match the words with similar meanings:

1. Yippee!   a. Hogwash!
2. Bull's eye!   b. Hey!
3. Baloney!   c. Bingo!
4. Shoot!   d. Hurray!
5. Yoo-hoo!   e. Fiddlesticks!

Q19. Which words belong with these opening phrases:

1. This food is horrible; _____   a. Yum!
2. I stubbed my toe; _____   b. Eeek!
3. I'm exhausted; _____   c. Yeah!
4. I just spilled something: _____   d. Whoa!
5. The food is delicious; _____   e. Grrr!
6. You're going too fast; _____   f. Pssst!
7. It's a mouse; _____   g. Whew!
8. I'm furious; _____   h. Oops!
9. Come here; _____   i. Ouch!
10. We won the game; _____   j. Yech!

Answers

Q16. 1. f   2. i   3. l   4. j
        5. b   6. c   7. d   8. a
        9. k   10. e   11. h
        12. g
Q17. 1. yikes   2. jeepers
        3. wow   4. gosh
        5. dadgum   6. golly
        7. shucks   8. dang
        9. gadzooks   10. heck
Q18. 1. d   2. c   3. a   4. e
        5. b
Q19. 1. j   2. i   3. g   4. h
        5. a   6. d   7. b   8. e
        9. f   10. c

Barking up the wrong tree

Give yourself 1 point for every correct answer: _____

A LITTLE HISTORY

- The German interjection, *hurrá*, comes from *huren*, which means "to rush." The Prussians were the first people to use the word **Hurray!** or **Hurrah!** as a battle cry during the War of Liberation in 1812. Since then, the United States as well as other countries have used the cry as a general cheer of support or approval.

- In American history, the word **fiddle** has always been associated with wasting time, as in the phrase, **fiddling around**. This idea came from the fact that fiddle players were usually traveling entertainers who didn't take life seriously. The fiddle then was considered useless and the **fiddlestick** even more so. As a result, **fiddlesticks** today means that something is of no worth whatsoever.

- The word **baloney** refers to bologna sausage, a mixture of different meats or byproducts that, to put it charitably, are not very specific. As a result, the expression **Baloney!** refers to suspicious, unreliable, and most probably false information.

- **To shuck** is to shell a mollusk or husk a vegetable and remove all the worthless pieces. In America, the exclamation **Shucks!** appeared in the early 1900s as a way to indicate that something was no good anyway. Today, **Aw, shucks!** is used to dispose of our disappointments, whenever we encounter the little troubles in life.

BORN IN THE U.S.A.

- Words such as *damn*, *bull*, *crap*, and *hell* have been considered profanity in the United States for centuries. But as America ages, so do attitudes toward words and their meanings. Today they are widely accepted as parts of everyday speech.

- Then we have curses with bizarre forms, the origins of which nobody knows: **Doggone it! Dadburn it! Dagnab it.**

WORDS OF WISDOM

"Everything is funny as long as it is happening to somebody else."
                                                        Will Rogers

Q20. Fill in the words that belong with these:

1. That's so sad; _____   a. Rah-rah!
2. Please be quiet; _____   b. Rats!
3. Something stinks; _____   c. Wheee!
4. Keep it up; _____   d. Ah-ha!
5. I blew it; _____   e. Boo!
6. Go, team, go; _____   f. Geronimo!
7. I found something; _____   g. Boo-hoo!
8. I'll jump first; _____   h. Phew!
9. I scared you; _____   i. Attaboy!
10. This ride is fun; _____   j. Hush!

Q21. Older Americans might yell a couple of these:

1. I'll be a monkey's _____!
2. _____ Jehoshaphat!
3. In a pig's _____!
4. Oh, _____ feathers!
5. Land sakes _____!

Q22. Be careful, only one word works:
1. And _____!   a. dog
2. Holy _____!   b. no
3. You _____!   c. way
4. Oh, _____!   d. doing
5. Gee, _____!   e. lizards
6. Jiminy _____!   f. how
7. Nothing _____!   g. betcha
8. Hot _____!   h. whilikers
9. Leaping _____!   i. mackerel
10. No _____!   j. Christmas

A foot in the door

Q23. Now burst out with a few *no* phrases. Fill in these letters first:

1. It's no _____ we lost; they're the best team around!
2. No _____ it's different on the moon!
3. I'd like to give you a ride, but no _____ do!
4. I had no _____ that you worked here!
5. We wanted to go to Vegas, but no _____!
6. Believe me; it was no laughing _____!
7. She's going to marry me—no _____ about it!
8. No _____, ands, or buts about it!
9. I want a relationship with no _____ attached!
10. He said it was no big _____!

a. D _ _ B _
b. _ F _
c. _ _ A _
d. S _ R _ _ _ _
e. _ _ _ D _ N _
f. W _ _ _ _ R
g. C _ _
h. _ _ T _ E _
i. _ _ C _
j. I _ _ _

Answers

Q20. 1. g   2. j   3. h   4. i   5. b   6. a   7. d   8. f   9. e   10. c
Q21. 1. uncle   2. Jumping   3. eye   4. horse   5. alive
Q22. 1. f   2. i   3. g   4. b   5. h   6. j   7. d   8. a   9. e   10. c
Q23. 1. f, wonder   2. e, kidding   3. g, can   4. j, idea   5. i, dice
6. h, matter   7. b, doubt   8. a, ifs   9. d, strings   10. e, deal

Give yourself 1 point for every correct answer: _____

A LITTLE HISTORY

- **Geronimo!** was a battle cry used in World War II by American paratroopers as they jumped out of airplanes. Geronimo (1829–1909) was an Apache Indian chief who led bloody reprisals against invading forces that moved onto his hunting grounds. The word is now a common cry of surprise or exhilaration.
- Some historians believe that **And how!** comes from the German, *und wie*, and has been around since the mid-1800s. Others say that it's either from the French, *et comment*, or the Italian, *e come*. Regardless of its origin, the expression sends the classic message, **You'd better believe it!**

- **Holy mackerel!** appears to be a sarcastic exclamation directed at Catholics who were not allowed to eat meat on Fridays. Since many ate mackerel, the fish suddenly took on a religious title. **Holy cow!** took on a similar meaning, as it mocked Hinduism.

WORDS OF WISDOM

"Don't change horses while crossing a stream."

American Proverb

ON YOUR OWN

1. *Translate **icksnay** and **amscray**. They come from Pig Latin.*
2. *When are you **going nowhere very fast**?*
3. *When would you use **giddyup**?*

SAY IT RIGHT

- In *Travels with Charley*, John Steinbeck talked about the fading American regional accents, victims of single-accent media and population displacement. He was sad, because small yet unique worlds loaded with unique cultural heritages were merging into one solid national voice and heart.

  What Steinbeck may have not considered is that America is a work in progress. While those regional cultures are disappearing, new voices are coming from all over the world, enriching and altering our language.

A LITTLE HISTORY

- American settlers often used bear, raccoon, fox, and beaver pelts for clothing, blankets, and other household materials, and each family had their own manner of putting the furs to use. From those early days comes the expression, **There's more than one way to skin a cat,** perhaps (we hope) in reference to a mountain lion. The phrase simply means that there are usually several ways to do the same thing.

- **Wishy-washy** originally referred to any watered-down drink, or a soup that was so watery that you couldn't taste the ingredients. Like **namby-pamby**, it now signifies weakness, lack of character, or general indecisiveness.
- In Dutch, a **honk** is a goal or home in little children's games. America picked the word up from its immigrants, and over time began to equate it with any feeling of safety or success. That is why the expression **hunky-dory** means all right or cozy today.

XXIV. WACKY WORDS!

Q24. Here are sentences to make with truly whacky words:

1. Behave, and quit your _____.	a. gumption
2. Come here, you little _____!	b. powwow
3. It takes lots of _____ to go to college.	c. roly-poly
4. She's sad and has the _____.	d. gobbledygook
5. That was a _____ of a party!	e. blahs
6. Staff had a big _____ with the managers.	f. clodhoppers
7. Their words sound like _____.	g. shenanigans
8. Santa's kind of _____, isn't he?	h. alibi
9. What's your _____ for missing the party?	i. whippersnapper
10. These _____ really hurt my feet.	j. humdinger

Q25. And these are some funny descriptions:

1. A _____ coach really motivates his players.	a. harum-scarum
2. That mountain over there is so _____!	b. gratis
3. I was _____ when the governor called.	c. yucky
4. He's feeling kind of lazy and _____.	d. namby-pamby
5. Your grandfather is one _____ old man.	e. itsy-bitsy
6. I did her a favor, so these tickets were _____.	f. lackadaisical
7. It's nothing but an _____ ant.	g. humongous
8. Sorry, but this food is really _____.	h. gung-ho
9. He's a _____ guy who won't speak up for himself.	i. flabbergasted
10. The drunk drove _____ all over the place.	j. cantankerous

Q26. How about a few all-American noises. Make sure they match!

1. Ding dong!	a. He knocked him flat!
2. Splash!	b. This tastes delicious!
3. Chomp!	c. The building blew up!
4. Bang!	d. My balloon broke!
5. Pow!	e. You're holding up traffic!
6. Zoom!	f. Answer the doorbell!
7. Ka-boom!	g. I'm taking guitar lessons!
8. Pop!	h. This water feels great!
9. Honk!	i. It flew right over us!
10. Twang!	j. The gun went off!

Answers

Q24. 1. g   2. i   3. a   4. e   5. j   6. b
       7. d   8. c   9. h   10. f
Q25. 1. h   2. g   3. i   4. f   5. j   6. b
       7. e   8. c   9. d   10. a
Q26. 1. f   2. h   3. b   4. j   5. a   6. i
       7. c   8. d   9. e   10. g

Give yourself 1 point for every
correct answer: _____

Puppy love

A LITTLE HISTORY

- **Namby pamby** was a nickname given to poet Ambrose Philips in 1726. Philips was known for his childish and cutesy lyrics, so the phrase **namby-pamby** began to surface as an expression for any childlike, weak, or indecisive behavior.
- **Gung-ho** is a corruption of the Chinese *kung ho*, or **work together**. The United States Marines adopted the expression in World War II, and it appeared in its original form, "*kung-hou*," as

early as 1942. The cry today has taken on a more general meaning, which is wholehearted enthusiasm, zealousness, or patriotic loyalty.

- The word **alibi** became popular in the 1930s due to Ring Lardner's short story entitled "Alibi Ike," which was about a man who repeatedly made excuses. The term was quickly acquired by the American public; however, instead of its original Latin meaning (*elsewhere*), the word was used to mean any excuse, pretext, or plea of innocence.

ON YOUR OWN

1. *Finish this classic:* **Peter Piper picked ...**
2. *Do you only* **hobnob** *with people who have* **pizzazz**?
3. *Have you ever seen a* **filibuster**?

WORDS OF WISDOM

"A penny saved is a penny earned."

Anonymous

"A penny saved is a penny."

Also anonymous

XXV. FOREIGN IMPORTS!

Q27. Over the years, many foreign words and phrases have become a
part of everyday speech, sending messages of their own:

1. She took a brief _____ from her job.	a. memorabilia
2. That guy is one tough _____.	b. passé
3. The players got into a _____ after the game.	c. résumé
4. I'm enrolling the kids at my old _____.	d. prima donna
5. Can I order the salad _____?	e. hombre
6. She acts like she's some kind of _____.	f. melee
7. That expression is so _____.	g. capita
8. She put on her _____ and went to bed.	h. a la carte
9. My dad collects Word War II _____.	i. mâché
10. I'll take my _____ to the job interview.	j. negligee
11. They made the mountain out of papier-_____.	k. alma mater
12. What is the annual income per _____?	l. hiatus

Q28. Stick with the foreign language:

1. I want the house, the family, the whole _____.	a. entourage
2. Let's ask the _____ to park the car.	b. verbatim
3. The tennis player had a full _____ of shots.	c. enchilada
4. I'd like to order the apple pie a la _____.	d. gesundheit
5. We got in a minor accident _____ to the show.	e. pirouette
6. Do you want to eat at our favorite _____?	f. bambino
7. She quoted him _____.	g. salon
8. Movie stars usually travel with an _____.	h. mode
9. I learned how to _____ in ballet class.	i. café
10. Let's take mom to the beauty _____.	j. valet
11. You sneezed and I said _____.	k. en route
12. He's been that way since he was a little _____.	l. repertoire

Q29. Now finish these off the BEST way possible:

1. The mystery guest showed up _____.	ricochet	blasé
2. I couldn't tell you _____.	entrée	serenade
3. The eulogy was given _____.	elite	adieu
4. She is gullible and _____.	por favor	heifer
5. It was boring and _____.	faux pas	silhouette
6. It was accurate and _____.	status quo	bamboo
7. You have style and _____.	incognito	per se
8. It's for the rich and _____.	vice versa	naïve
9. I'm going to bid you _____.	savoir-faire	addendum
10. Keep it the same and _____.	eureka	post mortem
11. Please serve the main _____.	apropos	coiffure
12. It was a mistake and a _____.	e pluribus unum	fromage

Q30. These become progressively more difficult:
1. Over the years, she became a baseball _____.   a. gondola
2. That politician has _____ around this place.   b. stein
3. She prefers to deal with employees _____.   c. boomerang
4. That topic is strictly _____ at the workplace.   d. moccasin
5. Have you ever gone on a _____ ride?   e. aficionado
6. My friend is a great _____ singer.   f. smorgasbord
7. We just bought a set of _____ furniture.   g. mano a mano
8. They're playing with a _____ at the park.   h. rouge
9. I picked up a huge beer _____ in Germany.   i. carte blanche
10. She puts too much _____ on her face.   j. karaoke
11. There was a complete _____ of food items.   k. verboten
12. Your other _____ is under the table.   l. rattan

Q31. For these, you'll need to unscramble some letters first:

1. She wore a _____ to the senior prom.   a. opeésx
2. He works as a _____ between two companies.   b. toorpupir
3. There was a _____ of items in the kitchen.   c. anbo dief
4. Did you see the _____ at the museum?   d. ecogras
5. He's a _____ professional in that field.   e. iniosal

Answers

Q27. 1. l   2. e   3. f   4. k   5. h   6. d   7. b
8. j   9. a   10. c   11. i   12. g

Q28. 1. c   2. j   3. l   4. h   5. k   6. i   7. b
8. a   9. e   10. g   11. d   12. f

Q29. 1. incognito   2. per se   3. post mortem
4. naive   5. blasé   6. apropos
7. savoir-faire   8. elite   9. adieu
10. status quo   11. entrée
12. faux pas

Q30. 1. e   2. i   3. g   4. k   5. a   6. j
7. l   8. c   9. b   10. h   11. f
12. d

Q31. 1. d, corsage   2. e, liaison
3. b, potpourri   4. a, exposé
5. c, bona fide

Hot dog

Give yourself 1 point for every correct answer:

BORN IN THE U.S.A.

- Are you aware how many words are foreign-born? **Bizarre, personnel, delicatessen, boulevard, vice versa, chef, potpourri, smorgasbord, czar, spaghetti, pizza, hamburger, falafel, brochure,** and thousands of others have been incorporated since the time of the Mayflower. Early American settlers often named places in other languages, and now we feel quite at home in **Corpus Cristi** (Christ's body), **Los Angeles** (the angels), **Baton Rouge** (red stick), and **El Paso** (the step).
- The same goes for major events on the U.S. calendar:

> **Cinco de Mayo**   **Mardi Gras**
> **Oktoberfest**   **Hanukkah**

- Native Americans have contributed to U.S. English, too. Besides simple items such as **chipmunk**, **tomahawk**, and **squash**, several states are actually Indian words: **Arizona** (small spring), **Connecticut** (long river), and **Michigan** (big water).

A LITTLE HISTORY

- For many years, **carte blanche** was the blank military form used to indicate an unconditional surrender. The phrase is now used figuratively to mean full discretionary power, unrestricted freedom, or literally, a **blank check**.
- The reason people call the college they attended their **alma mater** is because in Latin the phrase means **nursing** or **nourishing mother**. The name is appropriate, because this American institution of learning is responsible for "nourishing" the minds of its students.
- Contrary to popular belief, the French word **adieu** does not mean farewell, as in the expression, **I bid you adieu**. It is actually short for the phrase, **I command you to God**, which dates back several centuries.

ON YOUR OWN

1. *Are you a **Homo sapiens**? And do you have a **modus operandi**?*
2. *Guess the countries where these come from:*

   beef Stroganoff _____   **beef Wellington** _____

   pretzel _____   **goulash** _____

3. *Have you ever put a little **English** on a ball?*

Q32. Look how many English words come from Spanish.
Find the <u>one</u> that fits:

1. Be careful with the big bucking _____.	patio	pluma
2. Can you dance the _____?	colorado	corral
3. I'll need a _____ if it rains.	burrito	rojo
4. Professional bull riders work at the _____.	machete	siesta
5. We're going outside to sit on the _____.	hola	macho
6. Another word for donkey is _____.	chili	casa
7. Let's go, because the movie starts _____.	mesa	bronco
8. She was bitten by a _____.	loco	poncho
9. I cut through the bushes with a _____.	hombre	nevada
10. He has a ____ attitude toward women.	pintura	adobe
11. I'll take a short _____ this afternoon.	armada	libro
12. Do you want _____ on your hot dog?	burro	mosquito
13. We locked the horses inside the _____.	pronto	taco
14. Their buildings were made of _____.	tango	rodeo
15. He went _____ when I told him no.	amarillo	amigo

Q33. And this group has its origin in Germany:

1. We're doing an advertising _____ on the internet.
2. I think this old refrigerator is _____.
3. Would you please pour me another _____.
4. A wiener dog is actually a _____.
5. I learned how to read in _____.
6. It's ten degrees _____ in Chicago today.
7. Do you want mustard on your _____?
8. He sure is taking a lot of _____ at work.
9. A _____ engine is louder than a gasoline engine.
10. Do you know how to play_____?

a. frankfurter
b. kindergarten
c. pinochle
d. flak
e. lager
f. blitz
g. dachshund
h. kaput
i. fahrenheit
j. diesel

Q34. Let's not forget the Yiddish speakers:

1. I'd like a toasted _____ with cream cheese.	a. shtick
2. The event was full of _____ and glitter.	b. glitch
3. It took a lot of _____ to confront him that way.	c. mishmash
4. I was a clumsy _____ as a child.	d. kibbutz
5. I'm not interested in your sales _____.	e. schmooze
6. We found a small _____ in the system.	f. kosher
7. It's not nice to _____ about other people's lives.	g. bagel
8. There's a whole _____ of flowers in the garden.	h. glitz
9. He'll _____ with the boss until he gets a raise.	i. chutzpah
10. Their business practices aren't very _____.	j. klutz

Q35. These should be easy for you:

1. They raced down the hill on a giant _____.	a. ukulele
2. The _____ came when I won first place.	b. chaise longue
3. We broke up and made up, but that's _____!	c. voodoo
4. I'd like a decaf and a piece of that _____.	d. poodle
5. The _____ will be performing at 8:00 P.M.	e. poltergeist
6. I couldn't sleep, so I feel like a _____.	f. harem
7. Words like that were _____ in my home.	g. strudel
8. The creepy old house is full of _____.	h. coup de grace
9. He was sticking pins in a _____ doll.	i. zombie
10. We're running late, so let's _____!	j. taboo
11. Her little French _____ is named Fifi.	k. ensemble
12. He fell asleep sitting on a _____.	l. amore
13. They stayed at the _____ and went skiing.	m. toboggan
14. That Hawaiian guy plays the _____ and drums.	n. vamoose
15. I've got one wife, but the king has a _____.	o. chalet

Answers

Q32. 1. bronco   2. tango   3. poncho
4. rodeo   5. patio   6. burro
7. pronto   8. mosquito
9. machete   10. macho
11. siesta   12. chili   13. corral
14. adobe   15. loco

Q33. 1. f   2. h   3. e   4. g   5. b   6. i
7. a   8. d   9. j   10. c

Q34. 1. g   2. h   3. i   4. j   5. a   6. b
7. d   8. c   9. e   10. f

Q35. 1. m   2. h   3. l   4. g   5. k   6. i
7. j   8. e   9. c   10. n   11. d   12. b
13. o   14. a   15. f

Get the sack

Give yourself 1 point for every correct answer:

A LITTLE HISTORY

- For hundreds of years, Yiddish was the primary language spoken by the Ashkenazi Jews, and at one time it was spoken by millions of people of different nationalities all over the world. Although it almost disappeared by the 1950s, the language has been revived and is now being taught at several American universities.

- Historically, much of the United States once belonged to either Spain or France, which explains why thousands of English words have Latin roots. As a matter of fact, California's primary language was Spanish until the 1800s!

- German immigrants once filled the heartland of America, too. As a result, we continue to use words like **Dobermann**, named after Friedrich Dobermann (1834-1894), **Alzheimer's**, named after neurologist Alois Alzheimer (1864-1915), and **Levis**, named after clothier Levi Srauss (1829-1902).

ALL-AMERICAN CROSSWORD 5

Across

1. It was a _____ of the lip.
3. She gets _____ my skin.
6. _____ the time comes.
8. He's a good _____.
10. (means police)
11. Let's call it a ____.
12. Nothing _____, nothing gained.
15. You _____ my funny bone.
16. I was on pins and _____.
18. ___ my mother's grave!
20. She likes _____ rock.
22. (means "father" in Spanish)
23. I won't take ___ for an answer.
25. A rolling stone _____ no moss.
27. _____ many cooks spoil the broth.
28. He's a _____ and ready character

Down

1. Monkey _____, monkey do.
2. _____ the going gets tough…
3. Leave no stone _____.
4. Spare the _____, spoil the child.

5. Crime doesn't ____!

6. I felt like a fifth _____.

7. It's a dog ____ dog world.

9. She goes against the _____.

13. There's more than meets the ___.

14. He was _____ at the switch.

15. It hit me like a ____ of bricks.

17. _____ and the Tramp.

19. ___ and behold!

21. He ____ his eyeteeth on it.

23. She loves me ____.

24. To ____ is human.

25. ___ figure!

26. ___ far, ___ good.

A finished crossword is on page 243.

ON YOUR OWN

1. Where can you buy a **piñata**? A **chihuahua**?
2. Have you ever seen a **grotto**? A **regatta**?
3. Have you ever tried **Schnapps**? **Pumpernickel**?

WORDS OF WISDOM

"They spell it Vinci and pronounce it Vinchy; foreigners always spell better than they pronounce."

Mark Twain

WHAT'S MY SCORE?

TOTAL CORRECT: _____

TOTAL POSSIBLE: ___374___

Chapter Six

That's Entertainment

XXVI. FILM FEST!

Q1. No matter where you go in the United States, there's always someone who'll mention what's going on at the cinema. And can you
name a few classic films of the past? Fill in the missing word:

1. Gone with the _____   W _____
2. The African _____   Q _____
3. It's a Wonderful _____   L _____
4. Some Like It _____   H _____
5. A Streetcar Named _____   D _____

Keep it up. These were considered musicals:

6. Singing in the _____   R _____
7. West Side _____   S _____
8. The Sound of _____   M _____
9. The Wizard of _____   O _____
10. My Fair _____   L _____

Q2. Because they're easy, you'll need to add two words here:

1. One Flew Over The _____ _____
2. Terms _____ _____
3. _____ _____ Wolves
4. _____ _____ Patient
5. The Passion of _____ _____

Q3. These classics have proper names:

1. The _____ Falcon
2. Citizen _____
3. Driving Miss _____
4. Mr. _____ Goes to Washington
5. Kramer vs. _____
6. All About _____
7. _____ of Arabia
8. _____ Hall
9. The Bridge Over the River _____
10. Forrest _____

Q4. And what great films produced these all-American one-liners?

1. Hakuna matata …
2. May the Force be with you!
3. Phone home …
4. Play it again, Sam …
5. I'm the king of the world!
6. You talkin' to me?
7. Plastics …
8. Mirror, mirror on the wall …
9. You can't handle the truth!
10. I'll be back …
11. I'm mad as hell, and I'm not going to take this anymore!
12. Go ahead, make my day!

Q5. What movie are they talking about?

1. A sick son plays the part of his dead mother
2. A group is hired to eliminate mischievous spirits
3. A big mafia family gets revenge
4. A boy goes back in time to help his dad
5. A giant gorilla is loose in New York City
6. A sheriff has a gunfight at 12:00
7. A mad doctor creates a famous monster
8. A young man gets even in a chariot race
9. A small town lawyer fights racial prejudice
10. A giant killer shark is hunted down at sea

Answers

Q1. 1. Wind 2. Queen 3. Life 4. Hot 5. Desire 6. Rain
7. Story 8. Music 9. Oz 10. Lady

Q2. 1. Cookoo's Nest 2. of Endearment 3. Dances with
4. The English 5. the Christ

Q3. 1. Maltese 2. Kane 3. Daisy 4. Smith 5. Kramer 6. Eve
7. Lawrence 8. Annie 9. Kwai 10. Gump

Q4. 1. Lion King 2. Star Wars 3. E.T. 4. Casablanca 5. Titanic
6. Taxi Driver 7. The Graduate 8. Snow White
9. A Few Good Men 10. Terminator 11. Network
12. Dirty Harry

Q5. 1. Psycho   2. Ghostbusters   3. The Godfather
       4. Back to the Future   5. King Kong   6. High Noon
       7. Frankenstein   8. Ben Hur   9. To Kill a Mockingbird
       10. Jaws

Give yourself 1 point for every correct answer:

BORN IN THE U.S.A.

- In the early stages of **motion pictures**, people saw moving images in the **bioscope**. Then came the **biograph** and then the **movie house**, **cinema**, **drive-in**. **Picture show**, **flick**, **film**, or **movie**, whether it's a **box office hit** or a **double-feature matinee**, people have found them to be great places to escape from reality.

A LITTLE HISTORY

- In order to make the film, **Gone with the Wind**, 53 buildings were built, 1,100 horses were used, and over 550 different wardrobe items were created. The movie won ten Oscars and grossed over $75,000,000 in the United States and Canada. Released in 1939, the movie starred Vivien Leigh, Clark Gable, Olivia de Havilland, and Leslie Howard.
- The movie, **Frankenstein** (1931), was based on Mary Shelley's novel titled, *The Modern Prometheus*, which depicted Dr. Frankenstein's monster as some kind of superman. Actor Boris Karloff played the original role of the beast, and America has been trying to imitate him in sequels and remakes ever since.
- The classic film, **King Kong**, was released in 1933, during the middle of the Depression; yet, due to the elaborate advertising, it still earned $1,761,000 at Radio City Music Hall and Roxy theaters during its first run alone.
- Because of the overwhelming popularity of the **Star Wars** series of films, some of the characters have become part of all-American English. References to **Luke Skywalker**, **Darth Vader**, **and Obi-Wan Kenobi** still abound, even though they were introduced back in 1977.

?

ON YOUR OWN

1. *Who were* **Dr. Zhivago, Dr. Strangelove,** *and* **Dr. Dolittle?**
2. *Did you see* **Tootsie** *and* **Mrs. Doubtfire?**
3. *Name five films starring* **Agent 007.**

Q6. Figure out these one-word Oscar winners:

1. REVEBATHAR   B_____
2. TAPONT   P_____
3. ODARTILAG   G_____
4. RUVGEONNIF   U_____
5. GCAHOIC   C_____

Q7. How about a few classics
for the kids:

1. _____ Kids
2. _____ Alone
3. _____ Beauty
4. _____ Jam
5. _____ Nemo

Q8. Listen in as folks give
the classics a review:

1. I loved John Belushi in
   The _____ Brothers.
2. I loved Gloria Swanson in
   _____ Blvd.
3. I loved Yul Brynner in
   The _____ and I.
4. I loved Audrey Hepburn in Breakfast at _____.
5. I loved Burt Lancaster in From Here to _____.

Ghostwriter

Q9. Match these names with their common roles on screen:

1.	James Cagney	a.	private eye
2.	Boris Karloff	b.	ladies man
3.	John Wayne	c.	monster
4.	Humphrey Bogart	d.	cowboy
5.	Cary Grant	e.	gangster

Answers

Q6. 1. Braveheart   2. Patton   3. Gladiator   4. Unforgiven
     5. Chicago

Q7. 1. Spy   2. Home   3. Sleeping/Black   4. Space   5. Little

Q8. 1. Blues   2. Sunset   3. King   4. Tiffany's   5. Eternity

Q9. 1. e   2. c   3. d   4. a   5. b

Give yourself 1 point for every correct answer:

A LITTLE HISTORY

- Lives are changed in the landmark film, **From Here to Eternity**, as Pearl Harbor is bombed by the Japanese in December of 1941. Burt Lancaster, Frank Sinatra, Deborah Kerr, and Montgomery Cliff star in this movie that won eight Oscars, and was based on the novel by James Jones.

- American movie actress **Marilyn Monroe** was born Norma Jean Baker in 1926, and was married three times, the first at age 14. During her career, she became the world's most popular sex symbol, and after her alleged suicide in 1962, a true Hollywood legend. Her films include **Niagara** (1952), **The Seven-Year Itch** (1955), and **Some Like It Hot** (1959).

- Considered one of the most well-known actors in Hollywood history, **John Wayne** entered the film industry in the 1920s while working as a laborer on the Fox studio lot during summer vacations from U.S.C., where he attended school on a football scholarship. Over the years, Wayne's name became synonymous with action westerns, although he also starred in several World War II movies. His success and popularity rose throughout the 1940s, and by the early '50s he'd begun to produce and direct his own films.

ON YOUR OWN

1. *Name a film that starred* **Mr. Poitier**.
2. *Who was* **Mary Poppins**?
3. *Why did* **Johnny Weismuller** *scream?*

WORDS OF WISDOM

"Money is a terrible master but an excellent servant."

P. T. Barnum

XXVII. SONG AND DANCE!

Q10. As long as we're discussing American entertainment, we might as well mention the music. Let's start with some all-time favorites. Sing along as you fill in the correct words:

1. Home on the _____		HIGH	SAINTS
2. _____ Doodle		LAND	HILLS
3. Swing Low, Sweet _____		SMOKEY	RIVERBOAT
4. _____, Susanna		KNOW	DANIEL
5. Take Me Out to the _____		HEY	RIVERSIDE
6. The _____ Races		RANGE	MARY
7. For He's a Jolly Good _____		CORNER	MY
8. On Top of Old _____		WORK	YANKEE
9. When _____ Comes Marching Home		CHARIOT	JUMP
10. This _____ Is Your Land		RIVER	OH
11. She'll Be Comin' Round the _____		FAST	CAMPTOWN
12. Down in the _____		MICHAEL	SOLDIERS
13. When the _____ Go Marching In		TAKE	BALLGAME
14. _____, Row the Boat Ashore		LOOK	EARTH
15. I've Been Working on the _____		DOCTOR	FELLOW
16. Down by the _____		HIS	MOUNTAIN
17. Hey, _____ Me Over		JOHNNY	VALLEY
18. You Are _____ Sunshine		GARDEN	ROCK
19. Red _____ Valley		SAY	FAITHFUL
20. Getting to _____ You		DANCING	RAILROAD

Q11. You'll have to complete the whole phrase here:

1. Ain't she sweet, …
2. Row, row, row your boat, …
3. Buffalo gals, …
4. Jeepers, creepers …
5. Oh, my darling, …

Q12. Now add the missing lyrics:

1. I'm looking over a four-leaf _____ …
2. Eastside, _____ …
3. You ain't nothin' but a _____ …
4. What the _____ needs now …
5. Then I wish I was in _____ …
6. _____, Dolly…
7. John Brown's _____ …
8. Happy _____ to you, until we meet again…
9. Won't you come home, Bill _____ …
10. Fifteen miles on the _____ Canal…
11. Strollin' in the _____ one day…
12. He flies through the _____ with the greatest of ease…
13. My _____ lies over the ocean…
14. The old gray _____ just ain't what she used to be…
15. _____ keep falling on my head…

Q13. First unscramble the words, and then croon these oldies aloud.

1. Fly Me to the _____
2. Ol' Man _____
3. _____ Got Rhythm
4. Give My Regards to _____
5. _____ the Rainbow
6. Oh, What a Beautiful _____
7. I Could Have _____ All Night
8. When You Wish Upon a _____
9. Hit the Road, _____
10. Singing in the _____

NEDACD   RATS   INNOGRM
WOBAYARD   IEV   REOV
VIRRE   IRAN   NOMO   KAJC

Q14. This time, use old song titles as part of your conversation:

1. Great balls of _____! What happened to you?
2. Sometimes, you have to stand by your _____.
3. Show me a little R-_____.
4. This time, I did it my _____.
5. We're having a hot time in the old town _____.
6. Well, it looks like he's back in the _____ again.
7. I know, because I heard it through the _____.
8. They say there's no business like _____ business.
9. I've got to head up north, so I'm on the _____ again.
10. Goodnight gentlemen, and goodnight _____.

Q15. All-Americans know who made these tunes famous.
Name the singer:

1. Strangers in the Night   _____
2. Memories   _____
3. Yesterday   _____
4. Unforgettable   _____
5. White Christmas   _____
6. Jailhouse Rock   _____
7. Purple Haze   _____
8. Bridge over Troubled Waters   _____
9. Beat It   _____
10. Satisfaction   _____

Answers

Q10. 1. Range   2. Yankee   3. Chariot   4. Oh   5. Ballgame
6. Camptown   7. Fellow   8. Smokey   9. Johnny   10. Land
11. Mountain   12. Valley   13. Saints   14. Michael
15. Railroad   16. Riverside   17. Look   18. My   19. River
20. Know

Q11. 1. just a walking down the street
2. gently down the stream
3. won't you come out tonight
4. where'd you get those peepers
5. Oh my darling Clementine

Q12. 1. clover 2. Westside
3. hound dog 4. world
5. Dixie 6. Hello 7. body
8. trails 9. Bailey
10. Erie 11. park
12. air 13. Bonnie
14. mare 15. Raindrops

Q13. 1. Moon 2. River 3. I've
4. Broadway 5. Over
6. Morning 7. Danced
8. Star 9. Jack 10. Rain

Q14. 1. fire 2. man 3. respect
4. way 5. tonight
6. saddle 7. grapevine
8. show 9. road 10. ladies

Q15. 1. Frank Sinatra 2. Barbra Streisand 3. The Beatles
4. Nat King Cole 5. Bing Crosby 6. Elvis 7. Jimi Hendrix
8. Simon & Garfunkel 9. Michael Jackson 10. Rolling Stones

Glass ceiling

Give yourself 1 point for every correct answer: _____

A LITTLE HISTORY

- There are more than 2,500 cover versions of the Beatles' **Yesterday**, which makes it the most recorded song in history.
- Some believe the word **Dixie** refers to the area below the Mason-Dixon Line, but research shows a connection with the worthless ten-dollar bills issued in New Orleans. They were called **dixies** because the word for ten in French, "*dix,*" was printed on them.
- **La Bamba** is actually a traditional African song that can be traced back as far as the fourteenth century. It was picked up in Mexico after the Spaniards heard their slaves singing about the village of **Mamamba** in the 1800s.
- **Buffalo Gals**, published in 1844 with the title **Lubly Fan**, was actually a popular tune in minstrel shows around the United States. As a result, the song would change its name according to the show's location. Buffalo, then, refers to the city in New York State, and not the animal.

BORN IN THE U.S.A.

- Remember that many favorites, such as **Auld Lang Syne**, **Waltzing Matilda**, **Havah Nagilah**, **Danny Boy**, and **Ave Maria**, did not originate in the United States. Songs like these gradually became popular over time, as more and more Americans were exposed to them.

- Most major American plays and musicals have their premieres in New York City's theater district. These "Broadway" theaters (most are located on the side streets touching Broadway) are the supreme test: success means worldwide success, and failure means very quick obscurity. The cost of a Broadway production is so incredibly high that "off-Broadway" productions staged elsewhere in Manhattan or even Brooklyn are an important and complex art industry.

ON YOUR OWN

1. *Can you sing or tell the stories of either* **Old Ma Leary** *or* **Tom Dooley?**
2. *What did you find on* **Blueberry Hill?**
3. *What kind of* **eyes are smiling?**

Q16. Now it's time for some patriotic songs. Fill in the blanks:

1. America, the _____
2. God _____ America
3. You're a _____ Old Flag
4. The ____-Spangled _____
5. My _____ 'Tis of Thee

Q17. As an American, you should also know the Christmas classics:

1. Jingle _____   NAAGMR   DROWL
2. The _____ Days of Christmas   HATFULFI   PORULHD
3. Silent _____   GNISK   SLELB   VELEWT
4. Frosty the _____   GINTH   DREHAL
5. _____ the Red-nosed Reindeer   NANSWOM
6. Joy to the _____
7. Hark! The _____ Angels Sing
8. We Three _____
9. Away in a _____
10. O Come All Ye _____

Q18. With this set of Christmas tunes,
you'll need to add the last
two words:

1. Here Comes …
2. Have Yourself a Merry…
3. Do You Hear What …
4. We Wish You a…
5. Santa Claus Is Coming…

Go down the drain

Q19. More children's songs! Teach them a few favorites:

1. On a _____ Built for Two   B _____
2. In the Good Old _____   S _____
3. The Green _____ Grew All Around   G _____
4. Over the River and Through the _____   W _____
5. Just a _____ of Sugar   S _____

Q20. Now connect the popular melody with the film that made
it famous:

1. Talk to the Animals   a. Mary Poppins
2. A Whole New World   b. Dr. Dolittle
3. Over the Rainbow   c. Annie
4. Chim Chim Cheree   d. The Wizard of Oz
5. Tomorrow   e. Aladdin

Q21. Unscramble the letters. These are popular dances across the U.S.A.:

1. OFXTTOR   _____
2. ZLWTA   _____
3. AHC-CAH   _____
4. GWSIN   _____
5. OKLAP   _____

Answers

Q16. 1. Beautiful   2. Bless   3. Grand   4. Star, Banner   5. Country

Q17. 1. Bells   2. Twelve   3. Night   4. Snowman   5. Rudolph
        6. World   7. Herald   8. Kings   9. Manger   10. Faithful

Q18. 1. Santa Claus   2. Little Christmas   3. I Hear
        4. Merry Christmas   5. to Town

Q19. 1. Bicycle   2. Summertime   3. Grass   4. Woods   5. Spoonful

Q20. 1. b   2. e   3. d   4. a   5. c

Q21. 1. foxtrot   2. waltz   3. cha-cha   4. swing   5. polka

Give yourself 1 point for every correct answer:

A LITTLE HISTORY

- The song, **Over the Rainbow**, sung by Judy Garland in the classic movie, **The Wizard of Oz**, was almost cut out completely. Evidently, some executives at MGM thought the film was too long, while others felt that the song slowed down the action too early. In 1939, **Over the Rainbow** won an Oscar for best song in a motion picture.

- The words and music to **Jingle Bells** were written by James Piermont in 1857 for a Thanksgiving program at his church in Boston, while **O Little Town of Bethlehem** was written by Bishop Phillips Brooks in 1868 in Philadelphia, as he reflected on his trip to the Holy Land three years earlier.

- The melody to the **Star Spangled Banner** was actually published in England in 1780, but it gained popularity in America during the

War of 1812. After witnessing the bombardment of Fort McHenry by the British, lawyer Francis Scott Key saw that the American flag was still intact, so he wrote about it. Later, he added the English melody and had the song published. Although it was quickly adopted by the U.S. military, it wasn't officially recognized as the American National Anthem until 1931.

SAY IT RIGHT

- Some hit tunes were also movie titles, such as **Singing in the Rain**, **Fame**, and **Beauty and the Beast**.

BORN IN THE U.S.A.

- Whenever the U.S. goes to war, Americans always find a way to sing about it. Can you continue the lines from these old military favorites on your own?

  From the Halls of Montezuma …
  You're in the Army now…
  There she goes, over the wild blue yonder…
  As the caissons go rolling along…
  Anchors aweigh, my boys…
  Over there, over there…

- Songs like **The Yellow Rose of Texas** and **Carry Me Back to Old Virginia** were written with pride and affection for one's birth-place. Often, however, these feelings would bring about very chau-vinistic attitudes, disagreements, and altercations over which state was the greatest of them all.
- In this predominantly Christian nation, many religious songs and hymns have become classics. Can you sing these?

  Mine eyes have seen the glory…
  Oh, when the saints…
  Onward Christian soldiers…
  Amazing grace…
  He's got the whole world…

ON YOUR OWN

1. *Finish singing,* **Hail! Hail! The gang's....**
2. *How do you do the* **Hokey Pokey?** *The* **Chicken Dance?**
3. *What do* **Mr. Berlin**, **Mr. Rodgers**, *and* **Mr. Warren** *all have in common?*

WORDS OF WISDOM

"If you want the rainbow, you have to put up with the rain."

Dolly Parton

XXVIII. WHAT A LAUGH!

Q22. When American folks start to joke around, here are some things that make them giggle:

1. Telling		a. comedy
2. Pulling		b. riddles
3. Watching		c. pranks
4. Solving		d. fun
5. Poking		e. jokes

Q23. These sentences relate to American humor. Find the BEST word:

1. That guy can really deliver a punch _____.   a. stand-up
2. Did you hear about her April _____ gag?   b. glasses
3. I think I'll wear the _____ suit.   c. cushion
4. He thinks he's some kind of _____ comedian.   d. card
5. I loved watching the old Keystone _____.   e. man
6. I bought some Groucho _____.   f. fun
7. We gave him a whoopee _____.   g. fools
8. Do you know any good _____ tricks?   h. clown
9. I always have to play the straight _____.   i. line
10. We got lost in the _____ house.   j. cops

Q24. Look how often the word **funny** is used. Choose and
unscramble a word:

1. She was making funny _____ at me.
2. I've got a funny _____ that something's wrong.
3. Have you looked at the funny _____ today?
4. We'll send you away to the funny _____ !
5. That sure tickled her funny _____.

a. SPEARP
b. ENOB
c. IFEGLEN
d. CASEF
e. RAMF

Q25. Most Americans can complete these without any help:

1. Knock, knock. Who's _____?
2. Who's buried in _____ tomb?
3. Why did the _____ cross the road?
4. That was funnier than a barrel of _____.
5. Waiter, there's a fly in my _____!

Q26. Can you remember any all-time greats
of American comedy?

1. Charlie
2. Jack
3. W. C.
4. Lucille
5. Milton
6. Bob
7. Buster
8. Sid
9. Danny
10. Jimmy

a. Benny
b. Caesar
c. Berle
d. Durante
e. Keaton
f. Ball
g. Chaplin
h. Kaye
i. Fields
j. Hope

Go jump in the lake

Q27. Many comedians had their own T.V. shows.
Put the letters in order first:

1. Bill
2. Red
3. Bob
4. Carol
5. Jackie

a. ERAWNTH
b. TERTUNB
c. BOYCS
d. SAGONEL
e. TENLOSK

Answers

Q22. 1. e   2. c   3. a   4. b   5. d
Q23. 1. i   2. g   3. h   4. a   5. j   6. b   7. c   8. d   9. e   10. f
Q24. 1. d, faces   2. c, feeling   3. a, papers   4. e, farm   5. b, bone
Q25. 1. there   2. Grant's   3. chicken   4. monkeys   5. soup
Q26. 1. g   2. a   3. i   4. f   5. c   6. j   7. e   8. b   9. h   10. d
Q27. 1. c   2. e   3. a   4. b   5. d

__Give yourself 1 point for every correct answer:__

BORN IN THE U.S.A.

- Research in the arts has determined that everything in the United States, from religious hymns and folk dances through modern classical music and participation theater, came from other countries and has been adopted, adapted, and often transmuted. However, three forms of artistic expression evolved to such a degree that can legitimately claim the title **American**. These are jazz, striptease, and rock.

A LITTLE HISTORY

Reader beware. If you smile and nod with your head in agreement, you are showing your age:

- Early comedy on American radio, film, and T.V. included the great **Fanny Brice**, **Eddie Cantor**, and **Harold Lloyd**. Two of the comic duos that made us laugh included **Fibber McGee & Molly** and **Ma & Pa Kettle**.
- Even wooden dummies and puppets were used in comedy acts. During the 1950s, **Winchell & Mahoney**, **Edgar Bergen & Charlie McCarthy**, and **Kukla, Fran, & Ollie** were a few of America's favorites.
- During the era of silent movies, **Charlie Chaplin** (1889–1977) became known as the funniest man in the world. Amazingly, he wrote and directed nearly all of his films, and he composed the music scores for all of his later pictures that included sound.

- **The Marx Brothers** (**Groucho**, **Chico**, and **Harpo**) made a total of 13 zany comedy films in the 1920s and 1930s. The **Groucho** character was the most obvious, with his witty insults, long cigar, glasses, bushy eyebrows, and moustache.
- The popular T.V. show of the 1970s, **Saturday Night Live**, launched the careers of several comedians, including **Steve Martin**, **Eddie Murphy**, and **Bill Murray**. Weekly sitcoms, televised specials, and variety shows did the same for many others.

ON YOUR OWN

1. *Do you remember who played Barney on the **Andy Griffith Show**?*
2. *What was the name of the inspector in the **Pink Panther** movies?*
3. *How were **Rowan and Martin's Laugh-in** and **Hee-Haw** similar?*
4. *How many members did **Our Gang** have?*

WORDS OF WISDOM

"I don't know the key to success, but the key to failure is trying to please everybody."

Bill Cosby

Q28. The great ones also worked in teams. Connect the names that match:

1. Burns   a. Andy
2. Martin   b. Hardy
3. Amos   c. Lewis
4. Laurel   d. Costello
5. Abbott   e. Allen

Go to bed with the chickens

Q29. Fill in the blanks:

1. _____ and Mindy
2. The _____ Stooges
3. Spanky and Our _____
4. The Smothers _____
5. Laverne and _____

Q30. Connect each T.V. comedy with a classic one-liner from the old show:

1.	I Dream of Jeanie	a.	"You're going to the moon, Alice!"
2.	Gilligan's Island	b.	"I see nothing…!"
3.	Leave It to Beaver	c.	"Would you believe…?"
4.	Beverly Hillbillies	d.	"Good morning, Mr. Douglas!"
5.	Hogan's Heroes	e.	"I'm sorry, Master!"
6.	Get Smart	f.	"Princess, Bud, Kitten!"
7.	Gomer Pyle	g.	"Cut it out, Eddie"
8.	The Honeymooners	h.	"What's wrong with granny?"
9.	Green Acres	i.	"Golly, Sergeant!"
10.	Father Knows Best	j.	"That's OK, little buddy!"

Q31. Cartoon characters are part of our culture, too. Put the words together:

1.	Mighty	a.	Panther
2.	Daffy	b.	Bird
3.	Betty	c.	Coyote
4.	Wonder	d.	Fudd
5.	Pink	e.	Mouse
6.	Wiley	f.	Flintstone
7.	Elmer	g.	Bear
8.	Tweety	h.	Woman
9.	Fred	i.	Duck
10.	Yogi	j.	Boop

Q32. Which characters made these expressions famous?

1. Right-ee-oh! _____
2. That's all folks! _____
3. What's up, Doc? _____
4. Blow me down! _____
5. Good grief! _____

Q33. Americans love reading comic strips. Choose the correct character:

1. Annie…
2. Alley Oop…
3. Beetle Bailey…
4. Dennis…
5. Dick Tracy…

a. Teacher   b. Soldier
c. Cook   d. Detective
e. Zookeeper   f. Baby
g. Salesperson   h. Menace
i. Cowboy   j. Grandparent
k. King   l. Orphan
m. Caveman   n. Bus driver
o. Boxer

Q34. Now, try a few animals:

1. Alvin
2. Garfield
3. Winnie
4. Woody
5. Snagglepuss

a. Bear
b. Lion
c. Woodpecker
d. Cat
e. Chipmunk

Q35. Unscramble these letters to find some of America's comic books:

1. RAPNUMES _____
2. LKUH _____
3. AMABNT _____
4. HERAIC _____
5. PAECRS _____

Answers

Q28. 1. e   2. c   3. a   4. b   5. d

Q29. 1. Mork   2. Three   3. Gang   4. Brothers   5. Shirley

Q30. 1. e   2. j   3. g   4. h   5. b   6. c   7. i   8. a   9. d   10. f

Q31. 1. e   2. i   3. j   4. h   5. a   6. c   7. d   8. b   9. f   10. g

Q32. 1. Felix the Cat   2. Porky Pig   3. Bugs Bunny   4. Popeye
5. Charlie Brown

Q33. 1. l   2. m   3. b   4. h   5. d

Q34. 1. e   2. d   3. a   4. c   5. b

Q35. 1. Superman   2. Hulk   3. Batman   4. Archie   5. Casper

Give yourself 1 point for every correct answer:

BORN IN THE U.S.A.

- American television has dominated American media since its introduction to the public in the 1950s. From news, drama, and comedy to sports, cartoons, and talk shows, most of the entertainment and information received by American families comes from it.
- The list of great comedy on T.V. is endless, yet folks still refer to episodes or dialog from old shows like **Gilligan's Island**, **Happy Days**, **Sanford and Son**, **Cheers**, **Taxi**, and **All in the Family**. Other classics include the **Mary Tyler Moore** and **Dick Van Dyke** shows, **Welcome Back Kotter**, **Diff'rent Strokes**, and **The Jeffersons**.

A LITTLE HISTORY

- **Buster Brown** (1904) and **Mutt and Jeff** (1907) were two of the earliest comic strips in the U.S.A. Other classics that are still read today include **Moon Mullins** (1923), **Dick Tracy** (1929), **Buck Rogers** (1929), **Blondie** (1930), **Mary Worth** (1938), **Pogo** (1943), and **Rex Morgan, M.D.** (1948).
- **Amos and Andy**, played by Freeman Gosden and Charles Correll, were radio characters of the 1920s, 1930s, and 1940s. At its peak, their show was the most popular program ever broadcast, listened

to by nearly a third of the U.S. population. During the 1950s, the show appeared on television with African-American actors, but was criticized for their stereotyped portrayal.

- **The Honeymooners** first appeared in 1950 and was hosted by comedian Jackie Gleason. Gleason hated to rehearse, so in several of the scenes, he and the other actors would improvise on live T.V. The American public loved it, and by the time **The Jackie Gleason Show** premiered in 1952, **The Honeymooners** segment had become one of the most popular features on television.

Grab the bull by the horns

ON YOUR OWN

1. *What did you like about **Ozzie and Harriet**?*
2. *What's so special about **Mr. Magoo**?*
3. *Why did kids fall for **Gumby**? **Alf**? **Howdy Doody**?*

WORDS OF WISDOM

"Laughter is the shortest distance between two people."

Victor Borge

XXIX. FAME!

Q36. If asked to define Americans with one word, most people from all over the world will say, **Consumers**. Nobody else can produce, market, and sell so much and so well. Check *your* product knowledge.

1. I have to buy some more Kitty _____.
2. Could I borrow your Magic _____?
3. Today you'll need your Chap _____.

a. Saver
b. Bandage
c. Litter

4. Where's my Ace _____?   d. Stick
5. She'd like another Life _____.   e. Marker

Q37. The following names are also well known:

1. He took the Greyhound _____.   a. Detergent
2. Look at the new Shell _____.   b. Aspirin
3. You should try using Tide _____.   c. Watch
4. I can't find the Timex _____.   d. Station
5. She needs to take Bayer _____.   e. Bus

Q38. Match these words correctly:

1. Mack   a. washer
2. RCA   b. lantern
3. Kent   c. camera
4. Maytag   d. tennis balls
5. Kodak   e. lipstick
6. Coleman   f. towels
7. Wilson   g. cleanser
8. Scott   h. cigarettes
9. Revlon   i. truck
10. Ajax   j. stereo

Q39. Now fill in the blanks with the first word that
      comes to mind:

1. Schick   _____
2. Hoover   _____
3. Kleenex   _____
4. Clorox   _____
5. Colgate   _____
6. Simmons   _____
7. Huffy   _____
8. IBM   _____
9. Firestone   _____
10. Zest   _____

Monkey business

Q40. Unscramble these words to find five famous places in the U.S.A.:

1. _____
2. _____
3. _____
4. _____
5. _____

Center Square Grand Lincoln
Mount Memorial Times
Canyon Rushmore Rockefeller

Q41. Try some more:

1. _____
2. _____
3. _____
4. _____
5. _____

River Michigan Canaveral
Lake Hall Bridge Mississippi
Golden Gate Cape Independence

Q42. A few states have gained fame because they are part of song lyrics:

1. Deep in the heart of _____…
2. _____, here I come…
3. The sun shines bright in the old _____ home…
4. I come from _____ with a banjo on my knee…
5. I remember the night of the _____ Waltz…

Answers

Q36. 1. c   2. e   3. d   4. b   5. a
Q37. 1. e   2. d   3. a   4. c   5. b
Q38. 1. i   2. j   3. h   4. a   5. c   6. b   7. d   8. f   9. e   10. g
Q39. 1. razor   2. vacuum   3. tissue   4. bleach   5. toothpaste
      6. mattress   7. bike   8. computer   9. tires   10. soap
Q40. (Order will vary.) 1. Grand Canyon   2. Mount Rushmore
      3. Lincoln Memorial   4. Times Square   5. Rockefeller Center
Q41. (Order will vary.)   1. Mississippi River   2. Lake Michigan
      3. Cape Canaveral   4. Independence Hall
      5. Golden Gate Bridge
Q42. 1. Texas   2. California   3. Kentucky   4. Alabama   5. Tennessee

Give yourself 1 point for every correct answer:

A LITTLE HISTORY

- In 1907, James Spangler, a janitor in a Canton, Ohio department store, created a portable electric vacuuming device by using a soapbox, a broom handle, a pillowcase, and an old electric fan. Within a year, he was selling his **suction sweepers** to family members, including his cousin, William H. Hoover. The rest is history. **Hoover vacuum** is still one of the most common names in household appliances today.

- The **Greyhound** name was incorporated in 1930, and soon after, the company had motor coach franchises all over the United States. Even today, most Americans equate the word **Greyhound** with long distance bus travel.

- During the 1950s, improvements in research and development, as well as advanced mass production techniques led to the creation of the world's first inexpensive, yet reliable, mechanical wristwatch. Sales of the **Timex** took off in America, primarily because of the advertisements proving that the watch could survive any "torture test."

ON YOUR OWN

1. *What would you probably find on **Madison Avenue**?*
2. *What do **Piper**, **Curtiss**, **Martin**, **Falcon**, and **Cessna** have in common?*
3. *Have you ever seen pictures of an **Edsel**?*

Q43.   What familiar U.S. cities are they talking about here?

1. Emerald City
2. The Big Apple
3. The Windy City
4. The Big Easy
5. Beantown
6. The Big D
7. Motown
8. The City of Brotherly Love
9. Mile High City
10. The City of Angels

Q44. Now comment on some famous people in U.S. history:

1. Carnegie	a.	conducted nuclear research
2. Ford	b.	invented the telegraph
3. Edison	c.	worked on the telephone
4. Morse	d.	discovered electricity
5. Carver	e.	founded the nursing profession
6. Bell	f.	built a steel empire
7. Anthony	g.	developed the Model T
8. Franklin	h.	improved U.S. agriculture
9. Einstein	i.	fought for women's rights
10. Nightingale	j.	experimented with the lightbulb

Q45. And what great Americans said these things?

1. I cannot tell a lie…
2. One if by land, two if by sea…
3. I have a dream…
4. Four score and seven years ago…
5. Give me liberty or give me death…

One foot in the grave

Q46. Stay focused on your American history. Put a name and pick a letter:

1. Betsy **Ross (d)**	a.	The F.B.I.
2. Ulysses S. _____	b.	The National Anthem
3. _____ Douglass	c.	The Confederate Army
4. _____ Delano Roosevelt	**d.**	**The American Flag**
5. Teddy _____	e.	The Union Army
6. Robert E. _____	f.	The Declaration of Independence
7. John Paul _____	g.	The New Deal
8. Francis Scott _____	h.	The abolishment of slavery
9. J. Edgar _____	i.	The Rough Riders
10. _____ Jefferson	j.	The U.S. Navy

Q47. Some Americans have become legends. Fill in the first names only:

1. _____ Boone
2. _____ Oakley
3. _____ Appleseed
4. _____ Hickok
5. _____ Crockett

Q48. Complete these sentences correctly:

1. Lewis and Clark	a.	flew airplanes
2. John Phillip Sousa	b.	built a circus
3. Norman Rockwell	c.	fought for U.S. independence
4. Amelia Earhart	d.	hid slaves
5. Robert Fulton	e.	explored territories
6. Emily Dickinson	f.	wrote novels
7. Harriet Tubman	g.	drew illustrations
8. P. T. Barnum	h.	wrote poetry
9. Ernest Hemmingway	i.	navigated ships
10. Nathan Hale	j.	composed music

Answers

Q43. 1. Seattle   2. New York   3. Chicago   4. New Orleans
5. Boston   6. Dallas   7. Detroit   8. Philadelphia   9. Denver
10. Los Angeles

Q44. 1. f   2. g   3. j   4. b   5. h   6. c   7. i   8. d   9. a   10. e

Q45. 1. Washington   2. Revere   3. King   4. Lincoln   5. Henry

Q46. 2. Grant (e)   3. Frederick (h)   4. Franklin (g)   5. Roosevelt (i)
6. Lee (c)   7. Jones (j)   8. Key (b)   9. Hoover (a)
10. Thomas (f)

Q47. 1. Daniel   2. Annie   3. Johnny   4. Wild Bill   5. Davey

Q48. 1. e   2. j   3. g   4. a   5. i   6. h   7. d   8. b   9. f   10. c

Give yourself 1 point for every correct answer:

A LITTLE HISTORY

- In 1872, **Susan B. Anthony** demanded that women in the U.S. be given the same civil and political rights that had been extended to black males by the fourteenth and fifteenth amendments. Although convicted of violating the voting laws, she continued her fight for a federal woman suffrage amendment, organizing the International Council of Women in 1888, and the International Woman Suffrage Alliance in 1904. Although Anthony died before the passing of the nineteenth amendment, she is still considered one the great leaders in the suffrage movement.
- **Robert Fulton** (1765–1815), American inventor and engineer, is known primarily for building the first commercially successful steamboat to sail America's waters. A mechanical genius, Fulton designed numerous other devices, such as submarines and warships, and he also engineered a canal transport system that could operate with little water and on hilly terrain.
- During the 1600s, Boston was filled with Puritan immigrants who had been persecuted in England for their religious beliefs. Their way of life was strict, and included the banning of cooking on Sundays. As a result, the Puritan women prepared baked beans every Saturday, and served them for Sunday dinner. This is how Boston earned the nickname, **Beantown**.

BORN IN THE U.S.A.

- The lives and times of famous Native Americans, such as **Geronimo, Cochise, Sitting Bull, Hiawatha, Red Cloud, Pocahontas**, and **Crazy Horse** have been distorted, first to exploit them and then to obtain entertainment out of them. Only now is their cultural legacy beginning to be incorporated into mainstream society, and the impact of their languages to be assessed.

ON YOUR OWN

1. Who were **Paul Bunyan** and **Smokey the Bear**, and what did they do?
2. Why wouldn't you like to be called **Benedict Arnold**?
3. What do **Dolly**, **Eleanor**, and **Jacqueline** all have in common?

WORDS OF WISDOM

"The short memories of American voters is what keeps politicians in office."

Will Rogers

XXX. IN THE NEWS!

Q49. Why not reflect upon those events that have altered American history:

1. Revolutionary War	a. women's suffrage
2. Civil War	b. Mayflower
3. World War I	c. We shall overcome
4. World War II	d. Black Tuesday
5. The Great Depression	e. Napoleon Bonaparte
6. Spanish-American War	f. Boston Tea Party
7. Plymouth Rock	g. Blue vs. Gray
8. Louisiana Purchase	h. Remember the Maine
9. Civil Rights Act	i. D-day
10. Nineteenth Amendment	j. The Doughboys

Q50. These important people really made the news:

1. Howard _____ was once one of the world's richest men.
2. Neil _____ said, "One giant leap for mankind."
3. Jesse _____ was one of the greatest Olympic athletes in history.
4. One of the West's toughest outlaws was _____ the Kid.
5. It shocked the world when John _____ was assassinated.

6. Jackie _____ broke the color barrier in professional baseball.

7. Commander Robert E. _____ discovered the North Pole.

8. Dwight D. _____ was a popular general in World War II.

9. Charles _____ made news when he flew across the Atlantic.

10. Al _____ used to be one of the biggest gangsters in America.

On pins and needles

Q51. Match each event with the year it rocked the nation:

1.	Pearl Harbor	a.	1836
2.	Armistice Day	b.	1865
3.	Monroe Doctrine	c.	1968
4.	Watergate	d.	1941
5.	The Titanic	e.	1918
6.	The Alamo	f.	1912
7.	Boston Massacre	g.	1990
8.	Lincoln's assassination	h.	1823
9.	King's assassination	i.	1770
10.	The First Gulf War	j.	1974

Answers

Q49. 1. f   2. g   3. j   4. i   5. d   6. h   7. b   8. e   9. c   10. a

Q50. 1. Hughes   2. Armstrong   3. Owens   4. Billy   5. Kennedy
6. Robinson   7. Peary   8. Eisenhower   9. Lindbergh
10. Capone

Q51. 1. d   2. e   3. h   4. j   5. f   6. a   7. i   8. b   9. c   10. g

__Give yourself 1 point for every correct answer:__ _____

A LITTLE HISTORY

- Although the blowing up of the U.S.S. Maine in 1898 was one of the causes for the Spanish-American War, the navy's investigation of the matter never confirmed who was actually responsible for the explosion. In reality, it was the newspaper coverage in America that stirred up anger against the Spanish, and led to the battle cry, **Remember the Maine! To hell with Spain!**

- After Confederate sympathizer **John Wilkes Booth** shot Abraham Lincoln in his presidential box at Ford's Theater, he vaulted onto stage, cried *Sic semper tyrannis*! **The South is avenged!**, fled downstairs to a waiting horse, and made his escape. He was found two weeks later hiding in a barn, but no one knows for sure how he died there, since his body was never definitely identified.

ALL-AMERICAN CROSSWORD 6

Across

2. I hope I don't _____ the exam.
6. _____ makes waste.
8. ___ the nick of time.
10. The kids are playing _____.
11. They fell like _____.
12. She made a _____ catch.

14. I get my kicks on _____ 66.

16. On the _____ hand.

17. It was the _____ to the rule.

20. Please ___ still.

22. She really fixed his _____.

23. Over and _____.

Down

1. I'm not ___ liberty to say.

3. _____ are you're correct.

4. _____ safe than sorry.

5. _____ never strikes the same place twice.

7. We had an Indian _____.

9. It was a kangaroo _____.

11. They lost the _____ header.

13. She had Siamese _____.

15. I'll have ____ for the road.

18. Holy ____!

19. It knocked him down a _____.

21. She cut him down ____ size.

A finished crossword is on page 243.

ON YOUR OWN

1. *Did you hear about **Orson Welles's** radio spoof back in 1938?*

2. *Have you ever put your **John Hancock** on the dotted line?*

3. *During the American Revolution, why do you think they called them the **Minutemen?***

Q52. Complete these details concerning major events in U.S. history:

1. _____ became a state in 1867.

2. JFK was involved with the Bay of _____ incident.

3. _____ became a state in 1959.

4. My great grandpa grew up in the _____ Nineties.

5. My grandma was born during the _____ twenties.

6. There was a Gold _____ in California around 1850.

7. The Cold _____ was between the U.S. and the Soviet Union.

8. _____ was a ban on the production, sale, and consumption of liquor.
9. The book, *Uncle Tom's* _____, had a major impact on society.
10. Custer's last stand took place at the Little Big _____.

Q53. Here are some more newsmakers:

1. The _____ Trial in 1925 had to deal with the teaching of evolution.
2. Astronaut John _____ was the first American to circle the earth.
3. _____ Villa led raids into the U.S. from Mexico in 1916.
4. In 1955, Walt _____ opened his famous amusement park in California.
5. Lee Harvey _____ was arrested for the shooting of JFK.
6. The _____ were executed in 1953 for espionage.
7. Cassius _____ later became known as Muhammad Ali.
8. Dr. _____ changed parents' minds about baby and childcare.
9. Dr. Billy _____ became a respected evangelical preacher.
10. Charles _____ was arrested for the Tate/LaBianca murders in 1969.

Q54. And here's where America gets their news:

1. New York
2. Chicago
3. Washington
4. Boston
5. San Francisco
6. Wall Street
7. U.S. News and World
8. Time
9. Sports
10. T. V.

a. Post
b. Magazine
c. Report
d. Journal
e. Tribune
f. Illustrated
g. Guide
h. Times
i. Chronicle
j. Globe

Q55. These popular magazines are incomplete:

1. Good _____
2. Rolling _____
3. Vanity _____
4. Harper's _____
5. National _____

Answers

Q52. 1. Alaska   2. Pigs   3. Hawaii   4. Gay   5. roaring   6. Rush
7. War   8. Prohibition   9. *Cabin*   10. Horn

Q53. 1. Scopes   2. Glenn   3. Pancho   4. Disney   5. Oswald
6. Rosenbergs   7. Clay   8. Spock   9. Graham   10. Manson

Q54. 1. h   2. e   3. a   4. j   5. i   6. d   7. c   8. b   9. f   10. g

Q55. 1. Housekeeping   2. Stone   3. Fair   4. Bazaar   5. Geographic

Give yourself 1 point for every correct answer:

A LITTLE HISTORY

- The novel by Harriet Beecher Stowe, **Uncle Tom's Cabin**, sold 300,000 copies within the first year and helped raise awareness of the brutality of slavery. Abraham Lincoln even credited the book as being a catalyst of the Civil War.

- In 1888, a group of geographers, explorers, teachers, lawyers, cartographers, military officers, and financiers met at the Cosmos Club in Washington, D.C. to discuss the creation of the **National Geographic Society**, which has now become the largest nonprofit scientific and educational institution in the world.

- **Walt Disney**, an American icon, was launched into success after his 1928 cartoon, **Steamboat Willie**, hit the screen in theaters. By 1937, his full-length animated film, **Snow White and the Seven Dwarfs**, went on to gross nearly eight million dollars in its first release. Greater success followed, and by the early 1960s Walt Disney had become the king of American entertainment.

Paint oneself into a corner

WORDS OF WISDOM

"What lies behind us and what lies before us are tiny matters compared to what lies within us."

Ralph Waldo Emerson

ON YOUR OWN

1. *What do you know about* **César Chávez**?
2. *What do the names* **Rather**, **Cronkite**, *and* **Walters** *have in common?*
3. *Fill in the blanks:*

    _____ **Britannica**   **Webster's** _____   **Roget's** _____

    _____ **World Book of Records**   **Ripley's** _____

WHAT'S MY SCORE?

TOTAL CORRECT: _____

TOTAL POSSIBLE: ___422___

Chapter Seven

The Good Old Days

XXXI. DUTY CALLS!

Q1. The language of America has often been altered by the effects of war. Can you find the missing word?

1. Are you working today or are you off _____?   a. dog
2. My cousin just finished _____ camp.   b. boot
3. We spent hours over there digging _____ holes.   c. fort
4. You'll have to hold the _____ until I return.   d. duty
5. They put _____ tags around her neck.   e. fox

Q2. Do you know where the soldiers are? Join the words that match BEST:

1. latrine   a. lodging
2. mess hall   b. supply depot
3. barracks   c. brig
4. guardhouse   d. cafeteria
5. commissary   e. restroom

Q3. Connect the two halves of each military command. Select only ONE:

1. At   a. rest!
2. Carry   b. off!
3. Parade   c. face!
4. Fall   d. fire!
5. Forward   e. right!
6. About   f. on!
7. Seize   g. ease!
8. Count   h. arms!
9. Dress   i. in!
10. Present   j. march!

Q4. Finish up these other military expressions.

1. After we grabbed our weapons, Sarge told us to lock and _____.
2. I read that the officer was killed in the _____ of duty.
3. For her bravery, she was awarded the Purple _____.
4. It was great to hear "As you _____!" after standing there for so long.
5. As the first rounds were fired, everyone was yelling, "Hit the _____!"
6. The guard on patrol stopped us by yelling, "_____!"
7. We all stood at _____ and saluted as the general walked by.
8. I cried, "_____!" as I led my men running toward the enemy.
9. They play _____ at night and also at military funerals.
10. To get there early, the soldiers had to march _____ time.

Greyhound bus

Answers

Q1. 1. d   2. b   3. e   4. c   5. a
Q2. 1. e   2. d   3. a   4. c   5. b
Q3. 1. g   2. f   3. a   4. i   5. j   6. c   7. d   8. b   9. e   10. h
Q4. 1. load   2. line   3. heart   4. were   5. dirt (or deck)   6. Halt
       7. attention   8. Charge   9. taps   10. double

Give yourself 1 point for every correct answer: _____

ON YOUR OWN

1. *Have you ever seen a piece of **shrapnel**?*
2. *Do you know anyone on a **furlough**?*
3. *What is **reveille**?*

A LITTLE HISTORY

- **Lock** is an outdated English word for what is now called the action or receiver on a weapon. For the colonial American, it was called **lock** because the mechanism locked the hammer back in the cocked position. The trigger simply released the lock to fire the weapon. **Load** refers to the loading of the bullets, or with a musket, the charge and ball into the weapon's muzzle.

- During the Spanish-American War, U.S. sailors wore **boots**, which were high leggings to support their ankles and feet. The term **boot** soon became the nickname for any navy or marine recruit, so before they went to battle, they were required to receive their training at a **boot camp.** Today, the expression is used to describe a training program for any new or inexperienced employee.

- At a Union campsite during the Civil War, General Daniel Butterfield and his bugler, Oliver Norton, decided to revise the music for the "lights out" signal that was being played at the end of the day. The new call sounded that night in July 1862, and shortly, other buglers had picked up the tune throughout the area. What is surprising is that it also spread to their enemies in the south, and as a result, **Taps** became the official military bugle call after the war.

BORN IN THE U.S.A.

- Most Americans are familiar with military terminology. Are you?

    *My **drill sergeant** used to get free **ammo** from the **quartermaster**.*

- War veterans often comment about the various units in the military:

    *Our **platoon** was the best in the **company**, if not the whole **battalion**.*

WORDS OF WISDOM

"A good plan today is better than a perfect plan tomorrow."

General George S. Patton

Q5. Many words come from military life at sea. Unscramble these first:

1. All of his business practices have been above _____.
2. Everything seemed to be in _____ shape and good order.
3. Since the tragedy, we've kept the flag at half _____.
4. Unfortunately, we're all in the same _____.
5. The crew had to clear the _____ when the storm arrived.
6. If we didn't do it right, the captain lowered the _____.
7. I checked outside and the _____ was clear.
8. That really took the wind out of my _____.
9. She was a nervous _____ before the wedding.
10. He gets into trouble for being a loose _____.

a. mobo
b. kwerc
c. nonnac
d. lissa
e. pish
f. cedk
g. atob
h. rabod
i. samt
j. tacos

Q6. Now choose the correct verbs from the list:

1. This money should _____ me over until next week.
2. I expect to _____ a nice job once I finish school.
3. She tends to _____ her feelings of anger and resentment.
4. It looks like you'll have to _____ him out again.
5. At what time did you want to _____ off?
6. She's able to _____ off all kinds of facts and figures.
7. You shouldn't _____ in without knocking first.
8. I can't _____ what it would be like to be that rich.
9. He said he'd _____ the first person who crossed the line.
10. She's going to _____ over if she doesn't rest soon.

bail	cook
keel	steal
barge	hull
deck	sail
rock	land
fathom	sea
shove	bet
fish	tide
harbor	arm
rope	reel

Q7. Keep sticking in the words that fit BEST:

1. I had the chance to travel on her maiden _____.
2. Don't be so tough, and give him a little _____.
3. Don't worry, your _____ will come in someday.
4. It's a great opportunity, and I don't want to miss the _____.
5. If I don't get that money, I'm _____.
6. We welcomed her _____ when she arrived.
7. She tried to keep the business _____ until he returned.
8. We'll make plenty of _____ with this wind.
9. It looks like smooth _____ from here.
10. They had to batten down the _____.

a. afloat
b. hatches
c. headway
d. aboard
e. sailing
f. leeway
g. sunk
h. voyage
i. boat
j. ship

Q8. How about a few seaworthy commands? First fix the letters:

1. _____ as she goes!
2. _____ the deck!
3. _____ those sails!
4. _____ aweigh!
5. _____ hands on deck!

a. LAL
b. RHASCON
c. DSEYTA
d. AWSB
e. TISHO

Answers

Q5. 1. h, board   2. e, ship   3. i, mast   4. g, boat   5. f, deck
6. a, boom   7. j, coast   8. d, sails   9. b, wreck   10. c, cannon
Q6 1. tide   2. land   3. harbor   4. bail   5. shove   6. reel   7. barge
8. fathom   9. deck   10. keel
Q7. 1. h   2. f   3. j   4. i   5. g   6. d   7. a   8. c   9. e   10. b
Q8. 1. c, steady   2. d, swab   3. e, hoist   4. b, anchors   5. a, all

__Give yourself 1 point for every correct answer:__ _____

ON YOUR OWN

1. *Would you like to be a **castaway**?*
2. *When will an **enlisted man** go AWOL?*

3. *When does an officer scream,* ***On the double?***
4. *Have you ever seen the* ***quarters*** *on a ship?*

A LITTLE HISTORY

- The cannons of old warships had wheels so that they could handle the tremendous recoil after each shot by moving to and fro. But if one broke loose in rough weather, the heavy weapon could do irreparable damage to the ship. Therefore, it is understandable why the phrase **loose cannon** now refers to anyone who is completely out of control, unpredictable, and bound to cause another person harm.

- A **swab** was originally a mop, and sailors on the deck of a sailing vessel were often ordered to **swab the deck** to wash the ship clear of seawater. During the 1700s, not only were sailors referred to as **swabs**, but their superiors also were, because a navel officer's epaulets resembled the ends of a mop.

Poor as a churchmouse

- **Battens** are thin strips of wood that are nailed down to secure the edges of the tarpaulin over a ship's hatchways or **hatches**, that is, the openings on the deck. This was done frequently on long voyages, as sailing vessels would come across strong winds and rough seas. Nowadays, **Batten down the hatches!** is simply a general command to prepare for adversity ahead.

WORDS OF WISDOM

"Success is to be measured not so much by the position that one has reached in life as by the obstacles which he has overcome while trying to succeed."

Booker T. Washington

XXXII. WILD WEST!

Q9. Life in the Old West has left us with numerous words and expressions that still have meaning today. Try some of these, pardner!

1. six		a. post
2. trading		b. stable
3. tin		c. dust
4. livery		d. up
5. cow		e. horn
6. hoot		f. gun
7. gold		g. coach
8. wagon		h. poke
9. round		i. train
10. stage		j. nanny

Q10. Search for a word that matches up with each famous name:

1. Winchester	saddle	bank	ranch
2. Stetson	telegraph	soap	suit
3. Wells Fargo	mailbags	cattle	rifle
4. Western Union	knife	shirt	mining
5. Pony Express	hat	tobacco	foods

Q11. And who said the following one-liners?

1. String 'em up!	a. The cowhand
2. This is a hold-up!	b. The chef
3. Get along, little doggies!	c. The bandit
4. Get out of Dodge!	d. The posse
5. Come and get it!	e. The sheriff

Q12. Now choose the BEST action word:

1. The herd will _____ if you spook them.
2. I _____ that's the best thing to do right now.
3. It's time to _____ up some food for dinner.
4. They used to _____ for gold.
5. You can't _____ a man without a trial first.
6. The new owner needs to _____ all his cattle.
7. Where are you going to _____ down for the night?
8. I hope your horse doesn't _____ a shoe.
9. You'd better _____ on out of town.
10. She can ride side _____ if she wants to.
11. He went out to _____ me water from the well.
12. They like to _____ over the price of everything.

   a. throw
   b. saddle
   c. brand
   d. mosey
   e. fetch
   f. reckon
   g. dicker
   h. lynch
   i. stampede
   j. bunk
   k. rustle
   l. pan

Q13. Match each Wild West word with its translation:

1. fandango
2. red eye
3. grub
4. rattler
5. mustang
6. long horn
7. sarsaparilla
8. hoosegow
9. critter
10. saloon

a. horse
b. bar
c. jail
d. beast
e. steer
f. food
g. snake
h. whiskey
i. dance
j. soft drink

Answers

Q9. 1. f   2. a   3. e   4. b   5. h   6. j
     7. c   8. i   9. d   10. g

Pour money
down the drain

Q10. 1. rifle   2. hat   3. bank   4. telegraph   5. mailbags

Q11. 1. d   2. c   3. a   4. e   5. b

Q12. 1. i   2. f   3. k   4. l   5. h   6. c   7. j   8. a   9. d   10. b
     11. e   12. g

Q13. 1. i   2. h   3. f   4. g   5. a   6. e   7. j   8. c   9. d   10. b

Give yourself 1 point for every correct answer: _____

SAY IT RIGHT

- Not only are **cowboys** referred to as **cowhands**, **cowpokes**, and **cowpunchers**, but they're also called **wranglers**, **vaqueros**, and **buckaroos**.

BORN IN THE U.S.A.

- **Daniel Boone**, **Davy Crockett**, and **Jim Bowie** were just a few of the early American pioneers who represented the brave and adventurous spirit of immigrants in the U.S.A. Their rugged approach to exploration and homesteading was later exemplified by the cowboy of the wild South West.

A LITTLE HISTORY

- Beginning in 1860, daring horseback riders of the **pony express** began to carry United States mail between Joseph, Missouri and Sacramento, California, using relay stations that were set approximately ten to fifteen miles apart. However, the nation's first coast-to-coast telegraph was completed in 1861, so the famous pony express was actually in service for only about a year.
- **Hoosegow**, the old-fashioned term for a jail, comes from the Spanish word *juzgado*, which means *judged*. Since a poor Mexican ranch hand in the 1800s seldom had enough money to pay his fines or taxes, he was put in jail. After being released, he would return to work, explaining how he'd been arrested and *juzgado*. To Americans, the understanding was he'd simply been in jail.
- The first long-stage line was established between Scotland and England in 1670, but the **stagecoach** lines in colonial America didn't appear until the 1750s. Over the years, comforts such as cushions and springs were added, and by the 1800s, the newer six-horse coaches were gliding along at over ten miles an hour! However, like most modes of travel, the stagecoach gradually disappeared, as more people discovered that it was better to travel by train.

ON YOUR OWN

1. *What is a **Derringer**?*
2. *What words did the old **WANTED** posters usually have written on them?*
3. *Have you ever seen a **tumbleweed**? How about **chaps**?*

WORDS OF WISDOM

"Go west, young man, and grow up with the country!"

Horace Greeley

Q14. Pick the words that BEST describe these folks:

1. cavalry	a. dancer	b. preacher
2. marshall	c. cowboy	d. blacksmith
3. outlaw	e. Indian	f. lawman
4. wrangler	g. dude	h. soldier
5. parson	i. bad man	j. miner

Q15. Put in the first word that comes to mind:

1. The stage was pulled by a _____ of horses.   T _____
2. He was quick on the _____.   D _____
3. Cowboys wear _____ on their boots.   S _____
4. That place turned into a ghost _____.   T _____
5. The deputy just shot the _____slinger.   G _____

Q16. And here are some well-known Americans who made the West so wild:

1. Sundance	a. Earp
2. Black	b. Masterson
3. Doc	c. Cassidy
4. Annie	d. Jane
5. Bat	e. James
6. Wyatt	f. Holliday
7. Calamity	g. Kid

8. Butch   h. Bart
9. Jesse   i. Carson
10. Kit   j. Oakley

Q17.   When the cowboy went to T.V. and film, these stars became
         heroes:

1. J_____   Wayne
2. G_____   Autry
3. R_____   Rogers
4. G_____   Hayes
5. C_____   Eastwood

Q18.   Can you recall any classic T.V. Westerns? The letters are
         mixed up:
1. ETH ELNO ARERGN   _____
2. MEGKSNUO   _____
3. NNZBAAO   _____
4. HET NFRLEMIA   _____
5. KIVAMRCE   _____

Answers

Q14. 1. h   2. f   3. i
        4. c   5. b
Q15. 1. team   2. draw
        3. spurs   4. town
        5. gun
Q16. 1. g   2. h   3. f
        4. j   5. b   6. a
        7. d   8. c   9. e
        10. i

Pull the rug out from under

Q17. 1. John   2. Gene   3. Roy   4. Gabby   5. Clint
Q18. 1. The Lone Ranger   2. Gunsmoke   3. Bonanza
        4. The Rifleman   5. Maverick

Give yourself 1 point for every correct answer: _____

SAY IT RIGHT

- The Southwest was full of Spanish, because it was once part of Mexico. Try to pronounce any foreign words correctly:

  You are one tough hombre, amigo. You used your lariat to lasso the stray that was acting loco. If I were you, I'd take a siesta pronto!

BORN IN THE U.S.A.

- As you know, the Native American lived in the West before anyone else did. These are a few expressions that evolved when the two cultures clashed:

  If you speak with a forked tongue, it is bad medicine, and we cannot smoke the peace pipe. Let us send smoke signals to the other chiefs, so that their braves will not go on the warpath against the white man.

- Great warriors from nations such as the Apache, Cherokee, Arapaho, and Sioux fought bravely to protect their homelands. Over time, the white man's relations with "Indians" led to the adoption of numerous words into American English:

  Canoe, chipmunk, squaw, skunk, wampum, moccasin, Sasquatch, wigwam, papoose, powwow, squash, teepee, wickiup, tobacco, tomahawk, and **raccoon** are just a few examples.

A LITTLE HISTORY

- An **Annie Oakley** was once considered any free pass to a stage play. Annie (1860–1926), a rifle expert with Buffalo Bill's Wild West Show, shot countless holes through targets over the years. Similarly, theater managers punched holes through the free passes they would distribute.
- One of the first things that city dwellers had to do once they arrived in the Old West was to buy a new wardrobe. To survive,

they needed clothes made of thick, tough material, along with a sturdy pair of boots. Footwear was important on the frontier, and city dudes with their tender feet had to get used to walking around in the rough terrain. Today a **tenderfoot** is simply any novice, greenhorn, or person without experience.

- **Christopher "Kit" Carson** (1809–1868) was a famous American frontiersman, who became known as a skillful and daring hunter, guide, and soldier. People who knew him also described Carson as extremely gentle, honest, and wise.

- **The Lone Ranger** began as a nationwide radio show in the 1930s and was brought to T.V. in a series of half-hour programs in 1949. The masked Lone Ranger was actually John Reid, a Texas Ranger who had been shot in a deadly ambush and was nursed back to health by a friendly Indian named **Tonto**. In each episode, the pair solved crimes and fought injustice. Favorite lines from the program include **You, Ke-mo-sa-be** and **Hi-yo, Silver, away!**

ON YOUR OWN

1. *Texas Rangers left their mark in American history, but what do you know about them?*
2. *What happened at the O-K Corral?*
3. *What in the world is a chuck wagon?*

XXXIII. OLD ENGLISH!

Q19. Long before the Old West, Americans who spoke English used a lot of words that are no longer in use. Good luck with some of this King's English:

1. Our Father who _____ in heaven…
2. My country _____ of thee…
3. _____, the herald angels sing…
4. God shed His grace on _____…
5. God rest _____ merry gentlemen…

Q20. Even words from the early twentieth century are outdated.
For example, these refer to professions:

1. hoofer   D _____
2. flatfoot   P _____
3. sawbones   D _____
4. ambulance chaser   L _____
5. headshrinker   P _____

Q21. You may need to ask some old-timers about these, too:

1. He used to take his son behind the old wood _____.	a. petticoat
	b. kewpie
2. Her uncle used a _____ to make his own liquor.	c. telegram
3. Grandpa wore a _____ with his Sunday best.	d. trolley
4. And granny had to wear a _____.	e. castor
5. Their family traveled in an old _____.	f. derby
6. Sometimes they paid to ride the _____.	g. corn cob
7. He tried to win his sweetheart a _____ doll.	h. shed
8. The old guy liked to smoke his _____ pipe.	i. still
9. When they got sick, they had to drink _____ oil.	j. jalopy
10. To send a message fast, you sent a _____.	

Q22. If you enjoy watching old movies, these are for you:

1. A bootlegger sold his hooch in a _____.	a. shebang
2. That dame's a _____, and the guy's a louse.	b. oats
3. We gave him the _____ for stinking up the joint.	c. dirt
4. Have you checked out the chorus girls at the _____?	d. cooler
	e. burg
5. I'm really feeling my _____ today.	f. speakeasy
6. Give me the latest _____ on the new dish in town.	g. hood
	h. bimbo
7. The guards locked up the con in the _____.	i. raspberries
8. We were in charge of the whole _____.	j. burleycue
9. He went from big time _____ to a hobo.	
10. I'm from a quiet _____ north of the Big Apple.	

Q23. Here's gangster talk from the 1940s. First unscramble the words:

1. I'll _____ the next guy who moves!
2. They say you're on the _____.
3. Why don't you cop a _____?
4. I've got a _____ at your back.
5. He'll _____ for knocking her off.
6. Get my _____, copper?
7. He lost his dough at some _____ joint.
8. There's a gum _____ on my tail.
9. Don't say nothing to her, she's Lefty's _____.
10. Don't you dare _____ on our bet.

a. HOES
b. LMOL
c. SWHEL
d. PLIC
e. ALM
f. LEAP
g. GULP
h. YRF
i. FITRD
j. TEERHA

Answers

Q19. 1. art   2. 'tis   3. hark
4. thee   5. ye

Q20. 1. dancer   2. police officer
3. doctor   4. lawyer
5. psychiatrist, psychologist

Q21. 1. h   2. i   3. f   4. a
5. j   6. d   7. b   8. g
9. e   10. c

Q22. 1. f   2. h   3. i   4. j
5. b   6. c   7. d   8. a
9. g   10. e

Q23. 1. g, plug   2. e, lam
3. f, plea   4. j, heater   5. h, fry
6. i, drift   7. d, clip   8. a, shoe   9. b, moll   10. c, welsh

My ship's come in

Give yourself 1 point for every correct answer: _____

BORN IN THE U.S.A.

• **Candy stripers, cabbies, undertakers** are still around, but **soda jerks, organ grinders,** and **barbershop quartets** are a little tougher to find.

ON YOUR OWN

1. *Do you know any **baby kissers**?*
2. *Do you have **intestinal fortitude**?*
3. *Do you know what they used to do to **turncoats** at a **necktie party**?*
4. *Have you ever met a **hash slinger**?*

A LITTLE HISTORY

- The reason a police officer was once called a **flatfoot** was because in the early twentieth century, law enforcement officials had to continually walk their **beat**, which was the part of town where they were assigned. The word probably surfaced during the Prohibition era (1920–1933), when the general public was particularly contemptuous of those who were out there enforcing the law.
- A **still** is a vessel used in distilling liquids, especially liquor, and it often includes the complete vaporization and condensation apparatus. Short for the word **distillery**, this homemade device was once commonplace in America, particularly in rural areas where hard liquor was easy to make.
- The word **shebang** comes from the Irish word for an unlicensed drinking establishment, ***shebeen***. When an Irishman drank too much he'd often challenge others to a fight, which included everyone in **the whole shebang.** The expression now refers to any matter or concern. In English, a *shebeen* is called a **speakeasy**, because in order to keep the illegal business open, everyone had to whisper or **speak easy**.

WORDS OF WISDOM

"Nothing in the world can take the place of persistence."

Calvin Coolidge

Q24. We still use some of these old words today. Find the meanings:

1.	pants	a.	racket
2.	nonsense	b.	boner
3.	acclaim	c.	kicks
4.	police	d.	bloomers
5.	money	e.	kudos
6.	occupation	f.	gripe
7.	potatoes	g.	poppycock
8.	complaint	h.	loot
9.	mistake	i.	heat
10.	shoes	j.	spuds

Q25. And here's what you heard in the 1950s. Again, pick the BEST one:

1.	Bongo	a.	cat
2.	Crew	b.	rod
3.	Rat	c.	oh
4.	Dig	d.	box
5.	Jelly	e.	fink
6.	Juke	f.	drums
7.	Daddy	g.	ville
8.	Hot	h.	it
9.	Hep	i.	roll
10.	Squares	j.	cut

Q26. American English changed forever when kids started driving automobiles. Unscramble these car phrases:

1. His rod really hauls _____.		a.	GRAD
2. I bet you can't do another _____.		b.	ROLOF
3. You'll need to _____ the clutch first.		c.	YAL
4. Let's try to _____ up the engine.		d.	SNUB
5. She really burned _____!		e.	RYHERC
6. The _____ race lasted only a few seconds.		f.	OPP
7. My old man has a Caddy with a flip _____.		g.	BERURB
8. He likes to _____ it on the straight away.		h.	UPSO
9. Let's _____ a patch in front of the school!		i.	POT
10. Her car was in _____ condition.		j.	HEILEWE

Q27. Stick in the best word, baby:

1. We're throwing a _____ on Friday night.	a. gig
2. My new _____ doesn't pay very well.	b. spaz
3. She's got cash up the _____.	c. kookie
4. I was a total _____ in high school.	d. wazoo
5. He went _____ over the new girl in class.	e. bash

Do these without any help:

6. You're cruisin' for a _____.
7. Cool it! Don't have a _____.
8. You've got it made in the _____.
9. After while, _____.
10. See you _____, alligator!

Put the cart before the horse

Answers

Q24. 1. d   2. g   3. e   4. i   5. h   6. a   7. j   8. f   9. b   10. c
Q25. 1. f   2. j   3. e   4. h   5. i   6. d   7. c   8. b   9. a   10. g
Q26. 1. d, buns   2. j, wheelie   3. f, pop   4. h, soup   5. g, rubber
      6. a, drag   7. i, top   8. b, floor   9. c, lay   10. e, cherry
Q27. 1. e   2. a   3. d   4. b   5. c   6. bruisin'   7. cow   8. shade
      9. crocodile   10. later

Give yourself 1 point for every correct answer: _____

A LITTLE HISTORY

- The term **bloomers** comes from Mrs. Amelia Bloomer (1818–1894),
  who wrote about women's suffrage and became a famous lecturer.
  She always wore **bloomers**, which were long, loose trousers,
  instead of traditional dresses, and launched the trend in 1848 at the
  First Women's Rights Convention in Seneca Falls, New York.
- Although **Elvis** was **The most**, a number of others shook up the
  American music industry in the 1950s. They included **Bill Haley
  and the Comets, Chuck Berry, Buddy Holly, Richie Valens**,
  and **The Big Bopper**.

- **Drag racing** began in the United States in the late 1920s, when young people would race each other down the main **drag**, or highway, of their hometown. To avoid trouble with the law, car clubs were formed, and folks with their **souped**-up hot rods moved their races out to unused airfields and dry lake beds. Permanent drag racing facilities (**drag strips**) were then set up all over the country, and racing became a professional sport.
- **Bongo drums** can be traced to a certain style of music played in Cuba around the time that slavery was abolished in America. Originally, the **bonko** had heads that were tacked and tuned with a heat source. By the 1940s, when the instrument became popular in the U.S., metal tuning lugs were developed to facilitate easier tuning. In the 1950s, the drums became popular among the **beat generation**.

BORN IN THE U.S.A.

- Who is old enough to recall 1950s slang?

  Like, wow! What a drag!
  Cool it, man! What gives?
  Your pad, baby! It's square.
  I hear you! But I'm with it—check me out!

SAY IT RIGHT

- The word **cool** is around today, but in the 1950s and 60s kids would say **crazy**, **neat**, **keen**, **wild**, **swell**, **hip**, and **unreal** to express the same thing.

ON YOUR OWN

1. *Are you a **greaser**? A **party pooper**?*
2. *Have you ever **necked** in a car?*
3. *Have you done the **Twist**, the **Watusi**, or the **Mashed Potato**?*
4. *What was so special about **Ike**?*
5. *Briefly explain why the word **Sputnik** is so important.*

XXXIV. SINCE THE SIXTIES!

Q28. Most of the trendy expressions of the past few decades have come and gone, but are not necessarily forgotten. The early 1960s contributed these:

1. My dad's going to _____ me for this.	a. scene
2. I couldn't handle that crazy _____.	b. make
3. Let's sit down and _____ about it.	c. split
4. They had to _____ early.	d. cream
5. My kid sister saw us _____ out on the porch.	e. rap

Q29. Raise your voice as you read aloud:

1. _____ in there, baby!	a. give
2. _____ it out, bozo!	b. lay
3. _____ me a break, pops!	c. drop
4. _____ it on me, brother!	d. hang
5. _____ dead, odd ball!	e. cut

Q30. Now use some late 1960s slang. Find the BEST word:

1. That's _____ out, man!	a. burn
2. Don't put him _____, man!	b. foxy
3. She sure looks _____, man!	c. right
4. He tried to _____ me, man!	d. down
5. _____ on, man!	e. far

Q31. Now, what's happening here?

1. _____ me some skin!	a. spare
2. You need to _____ out.	b. slide
3. _____ me some bread.	c. streak
4. I've got to _____ before twelve.	d. mellow
5. Let's _____ at the concert!	e. book

Q32. And these exclamations are 1960s classics:

1. TAGSUTHOIT!   _____
2. SOBS!   _____
3. DILSO!   _____
4. YOGORV!   _____
5. CLEIPEHSCYD!   _____

Q33. Create the full names of these folks who stood out during the sixties:

1. _____ Lennon
2. _____ Luther King, Jr.
3. _____ Fonda
4. John F. _____
5. _____ Leary
6. _____ Baez
7. _____ Joplin
8. Malcolm _____
9. Ho Chi _____
10. _____ Sullivan
11. _____ Hendrix
12. Richard Milhous _____

Rat race

Q34. Link each place with a well-known event from the past:

1. Kent State   a. outdoor concert
2. Haight-Ashbury   b. race riots
3. Woodstock   c. Watergate
4. Selma   d. student shootings
5. Washington D.C.   e. hippie haven

Answers

Q28. 1. d   2. a   3. e   4. c   5. b
Q29. 1. d   2. e   3. a   4. b   5. c
Q30. 1. e   2. d   3. b   4. a   5. c
Q31. 1. b   2. d   3. a   4. e   5. c
Q32. 1. outtasight   2. boss   3. solid   4. groovy   5. psychedelic
Q33. 1. John   2. Martin   3. Jane   4. Kennedy   5. Timothy   6. Joan
        7. Janis   8. X   9. Minh   10. Ed   11. Jimi   12. Nixon
Q34. 1. d   2. e   3. a   4. b   5. c

Give yourself 1 point for every correct answer:

A LITTLE HISTORY

- The **hippie movement** began right after World War II, when disillu-sioned young people began to question the **Establishment** and society's values. The **Beat Generation** with its **beatniks** came first, as they used poetry, music, and art to express themselves. Refusing to conform, they spoke **hip** language to communicate with one another. By the 1960s, these **hipsters,** or **hippies,** were taking their message out of the coffee shops and onto school campuses and streets.

- **Malcolm X** was a black militant leader who articulated the con-cepts of racial pride and black nationalism in the early 1960s. Until his assassination in 1965, he was the voice for the Nation of Islam, the faith of many Black Muslims in America today.

- Folk singer **Joan Baez** became a hit in the 1960s because of the political messages she communicated through her music. She was also involved in several social causes, including civil rights and non-violence, and was sometimes jailed for her participation in the protests. Later, however, Baez added country western songs to her repertoire, and focused on more mainstream music.

- The relationship between **groove** and music probably stems from the old-fashioned phonograph, which played musical records made of circular **grooves.** This concept associated **in the groove** with vibrations or moving with the flow. The word **groovy** came later, and was quickly equated with **smooth**, **all right**, or **totally cool**.

BORN IN THE U.S.A.

- If you smile with these, you are showing your age:

    I was a flag-burning draft dodger during the Tet Offensive in 'Nam. I believed in sex, drugs, and rock and roll. I turned on, tuned in, and dropped out.

    As a kid, I loved Bob Dylan, but my favorite groups were the Beatles and the Stones. I also had albums by the Airplane, Zeppelin, Buffalo Springfield, and Credence. Today, I listen to the oldies on the radio.

ON YOUR OWN

1. *Have you ever owned **black lights**?*
2. *Can you sing **Tiptoe through the Tulips**? Who made it famous?*
3. *Tell which **Apollo** flight reached the moon first.*

Q35. Move into the late 1960s with this new set of expressions:

1. flower	a. protest
2. peace	b. trip
3. birth	c. boots
4. acid	d. glasses
5. mini	e. control
6. folk	f. dye
7. antiwar	g. skirt
8. granny	h. sign
9. tie	i. power
10. go-go	j. music
11. transistor	k. bug
12. VW	l. radio

Q36. Choose the best action word:

1. She _____ him for another guy.
2. I _____ out when I got the good news.
3. That movie totally _____ me away.
4. He's _____ that he didn't get the job.
5. They always get _____ up before the game.

a. blew
b. bummed
c. psyched
d. dumped
e. flipped

Q37. And then we moved into 1970s English:

1. You'll get _____ if you work out a lot.
2. That liar gave me a _____ excuse.
3. His bathroom was smelly and _____.
4. It was a little too hot and _____ for me.
5. She was _____ that she won first place.

a. stoked
b. gross
c. heavy
d. buff
e. bogus

Q38. Remember these? Fill in the missing word:

1. _____ sure!
2. Like, oh my _____!
3. _____ me with a spoon!
4. Chill _____!
5. As _____!

Q39. Make these letters form 1980s words that express a positive response:

1. AMESWEO   _____
2. LERLIK   _____
3. ROAMJ   _____
4. ABD   _____
5. LASERTL   _____
6. LARBTUU   _____
7. KDEIWC   _____
8. DRA   _____
9. NEELCTELX   _____
10. YLF   _____

Ambulance chaser

Q40. The 1990s and the new millennium brought about the following, but no one is sure how long they'll stay in circulation:

1. That's outdated; it's so _____ school.   O _____
2. I messed up; it was _____.   B _____
3. Props to you; you _____, girl!   G _____
4. Don't be a whacko; don't go _____ on me!   P _____
5. He was in my face; he was up in my _____.   G _____

Q41. Insert the first word that comes to mind:

1. Could you please page me on my _____?
2. We're working twenty-four- _____.
3. She loves driving her new S _____.
4. Are you sure that book is politically _____?
5. She's decided to be a stay-at-_____ mom.
6. I'm always using my hands-free _____.
7. You need to get in touch with your inner _____.
8. Who'll be the designated _____?
9. I got a virus and my _____ crashed.
10. Come on over and watch the game on my new big _____.

Answers

Q35. 1. i   2. h   3. e   4. b   5. g   6. j   7. a   8. d   9. f   10. c
      11. l   12. k

Q36. 1. d   2. e   3. a   4. b   5. c

Q37. 1. d   2. e   3. b   4. c   5. a

Q38. 1. for   2. God   3. gag   4. out   5. if

Q39. 1. awesome   2. killer   3. major   4. bad   5. stellar   6. tubular
      7. wicked   8. rad   9. excellent   10. fly

Q40. 1. old   2. bad   3. go   4. postal   5. grill

Q41. 1. beeper   2. seven   3. UV   4. correct   5. home   6. phone
      7. child   8. driver   9. computer   10. screen

Give yourself 1 point for every correct answer:

SAY IT RIGHT'

- An American pattern is to shorten words if you can:

    Stop dissing the temp who just fessed up about taking the CDs.

    (Stop being disrespectful to the temporary employee who just confessed about taking the compact discs.)
- For generations, young Americans have discovered their own unique set of vocabulary:

    Duh! I'm all like, "hello?"
    Shut up, dude!
    Yes way.

BORN IN THE U.S.A.

- Ever since the computer/internet age began, Americans have been talking about *websites, dot-coms, screensavers, laptops, chat rooms,* and *search engines*. New *techno-babble* seems to surface everyday, so it's hard to say if it will ever achieve all-American status.
- Young folks are always finding new ways of expressing their approval of something. Here are a few words from recent history:

    It's slammin', the bomb, sweet, phat, tight, smooth, and *dope!*

- From *CB Talk* to *Country Western* and from *Disco Dancing* to *Miami Vice*, the 1970s and 1980s flowed from one funky trend to the next. The 1990s brought us *rap music, soccer moms, cell phones,* and *Nintendo,* and today in the early 2000s, plenty of new trends continue. One consistent pattern, however, is that Americans are really into name-calling:

    That redneck jarhead is totally lame and clueless. He's a nerd, a geek, a dweeb, a dork, and a total dufus!

- *Political correctness* is now an active part of American English, but most folks still haven't figured it out yet:

    Am I *White* or *Anglo*? Is she *Black* or *African-American*? Are they *Spanish*, *Latino*, or *Hispanic*?

A LITTLE HISTORY

- During the 1960s, **go-go boots** were calf-level boots that came in bright white leather or vinyl, and had a broad heel. They originated from the collection of Parisian Andre Courreges, but were made famous by Nancy Sinatra's hit, **"These Boots Are Made for Walking"** in 1965.
- The first pager-like system in the U.S. was used in 1921 by the Detroit Police Department, but the term **pager** wasn't used until 1959. The first pager similar to the kind we have today was the Motorola Pageboy I, introduced in 1974. By 1980, there were 3.2 million pager users worldwide, and by 1994 there were over 61 million.
- During the 1980s, a number of films, hit songs, and television programs introduced American youth to new slang expressions that originated in California. For example, **Valley Girl English** added phrases like, **gag me with a spoon** and **totally**, while **Surf Talk English** contributed words such as **tubular** and **buff**.

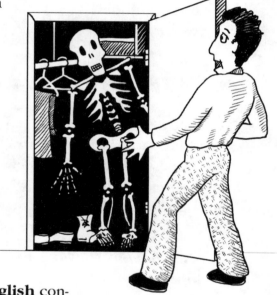

Skeleton in the closet

ON YOUR OWN

1. *Are your friends **preppies**, **baby boomers**, or **Gen Xers**?*
2. *Have you ever watched a **chick flick**?*
3. *Do you know anyone with **love handles**?*

XXXV. MORE, MORE, MORE!

Q42. Let's finish up with a mixed bag of this author's favorite words and expressions. The words you use should *end* in the letters shown at right:

1. Unfortunately, he has a very _____ fuse.	_____T
2. Let's try to make a last _____ effort.	_____H
3. Trust me; she's the _____ article.	_____E
4. Do you recall the words to your fight _____ in high school?	_____G
5. That's a little hard for me to _____.	_____W
6. I don't believe there was any _____ will.	_____L
7. It hit me like a _____ of bricks.	_____N
8. Don't try to sweep it under the _____.	_____G
9. Listen pal, I wasn't born _____.	_____Y
10. We think she should have a _____ shake.	_____R
11. I'm trying to follow in his _____.	_____S
12. It looks like all _____ are go.	_____S
13. My grandma's got a _____ of gold.	_____T
14. I believe it's true beyond a shadow of a _____.	_____T
15. She looks at the _____ through rose-colored glasses.	_____D

Q43. Keep going, but use the word list found below:

> LOSS TIDY BODY FLYING GALORE
> UNDERDOG STICKS MOONLIGHT HOT SWEAT
> TOTALED DIME MAROONED SAVVY LIGHT

1. He had to _____ in order to get the cash.
2. I think I'll _____ up before she gets here.
3. She _____ her car over the weekend.
4. That job was no _____.
5. I'm at a _____ for words.
6. He's a very _____ character.
7. There was food _____ at the party.
8. They were _____ on a deserted island.

9. Let's trip the _____ fantastic.
10. She passed with _____ colors.
11. The police were in _____ pursuit.
12. We always cheer for the _____.
13. He lives way out there in the _____.
14. This sucker stops on a _____.
15. Those guys are really into _____ building.

Q44. Now, mention more well-known places in the U.S.A.:

1. Which National Park features Old Faithful?
2. Which city presents opera at the Met?
3. Which state has the Everglades?
4. Which city has the Smithsonian Institution?
5. Which state is known for the Rockies?

Q45. And here are other famous Americans. Make the proper connection:

1. B. F. Goodrich
2. J. C. Penny
3. Eli Whitney
4. Booker T. Washington
5. Columbus
6. Jack Dempsey
7. Clara Barton
8. J. P. Morgan
9. Thomas Paine
10. Stonewall Jackson

a. The Red Cross
b. Extreme wealth
c. The Civil War
d. Boxing champ
e. The cotton gin
f. Independence
g. Automobile tires
h. Niña, Pinta, and Santa María
i. Department stores
j. Tuskeegee Institute

Q46. Answer these trivia questions as briefly as possible:

1. What town is famous for its witch trials?   _____
2. Which president is famous for being raised in a log cabin?   _____
3. What did David Crockett wear on his head?   _____
4. Lady Liberty is on which island?   _____
5. Who was Tom Sawyer's sidekick?   _____

6. What is America's most popular bikers club? _____

7. What's the highest badge in Boy Scouts? _____

8. What rights must be read when someone is arrested? _____

9. What's the law that says things will probably go wrong? _____

10. Where has the U.S. traditionally kept its gold reserves? _____

Answers

Q42. 1. short 2. ditch
   3. genuine 4. song
   5. swallow 6. ill
   7. ton 8. rug
   9. yesterday 10. fair
   11. footsteps
   12. systems 13. heart
   14. doubt 15. world

Q43. 1. moonlight 2. tidy
   3. totaled 4. sweat
   5. loss 6. savvy
   7. galore 8. marooned
   9. light 10. flying
   11. hot 12. underdog
   13. sticks 14. dime 15. body

Snake in the grass

Q44. 1. Yellowstone 2. New York 3. Florida 4. Washington, D.C.
   5. Colorado

Q45. 1. g 2. i 3. e 4. j 5. h 6. d 7. a 8. b 9. f 10. c

Q46. 1. Salem 2. Lincoln 3. Coonskin Cap 4. Ellis 5. Huck Finn
   6. Hell's Angels 7. The Eagle 8. Miranda 9. Murphy's Law
   10. Fort Knox

Give yourself 1 point for every correct answer: _____

BORN IN THE U.S.A.

- Americans still hold onto the classic one-liners in formal letter writing:

  To Whom It May Concern, Dear Sirs, Sincerely, Yours Truly

- The U.S. is a generous country. **Easter Seals, Boys and Girls Clubs, the Jerry Lewis Telethon, the Salvation Army**, and the **American Cancer Society** have prospered and grown.

A LITTLE HISTORY

- In battles during World War I, men primarily fought out of trenches or ditches. If their trench was heavily bombed or being overrun by the enemy, they'd retreat to previously dug ditches. Eventually, however, they'd come to the final trench, where they were forced to make a **last ditch** effort to hold the line. This expression of desperation has a very similar meaning today.
- Before vacuum cleaners or wall-to-wall carpeting, the wooden floors of a home had to be swept regularly with a broom, throwaway rugs had to be aired out, and furniture had to be moved, so it was not an easy job. However, if a person was in a lazy mood, the dirt remained, because he or she would simply **sweep it under the rug**. The expression still means to cover up or conceal something disagreeable or embarrassing.
- Dog fighting was once a popular sport on the American frontier. In dog fighting, the key was to conquer the top position, in order to overpower the one underneath. Sometimes the **top-dog** would make a wrong move, and the **underdog** was able to reverse the situation and take control. Like the animal, the top dog of today occupies a dominant position in any enterprise, whereas the underdog is anyone who is at a disadvantage in life, or finds himself in an inferior position.

ALL-AMERICAN CROSSWORD 7

Across

1. Been there, done _____.
3. It'll be _____ and go from here.
6. He's just another _____ polisher.
10. Her _____ is in the right place.
12. I had to _____ over backwards.
13. (Means early 20th-century show)
14. The ex-con tried to _____ bail.
16. ____, ____ , ____ for the home team!
17. She's scared the _____ daylights out of me.
18. He's Johnny-___-the-spot.
19. That's the _____ and the short of it.
21. Live and ____ live.
22. I'll never get _____ to it.

Down

1. Here's a word ___ the wise!
2. Ta-___, good-bye!
3. You really ____ me off!
4. Let's live it ___.
5. The _____ is on the wall.

7. Take your _____ everybody!
8. He's just a _____ pig.
9. The cat has nine _____.
11. She's skating on ____ ice.
12. You've bats in the _____.
15. We won _____ down.
18. ___ your marks…
20. Not for love ___ money.

A finished crossword is on page 244.

Q47. Most Americans have spent a good part of their lives watching television, so these should be easy:

1. Who's on *Monday Night* _____?
2. I heard about it on _____ *Minutes*.
3. *The Price Is Right* and *Jeopardy* are my two favorite _____ shows.
4. Ed McMahon used to say, Heeere's _____!
5. The Muppets became famous on _____ *Street*.
6. *Dragnet* takes place in the city of _____.
7. Uncle Fester is a member of the _____ *Family*.
8. Smile, you're on _____!
9. I feel like I'm in the *Twilight* _____.
10. The Vice President appeared on _____ *the Press*.

Flower power.

Q48. Match the products from the list below with these classic commercials:

> BOUNTY   UNITED   LIFE CALL MED ALERT
> MAXWELL HOUSE   NESTLE'S   RICE KRISPIES   OREO
> ENERGIZER   WINDEX   PEPSI   CREST   ALLSTATE
> MILLER   TYLENOL   ALKA-SELTZER   NIKE
> WENDY'S   RITZ   TWINNING'S   CHEERIOS   FORD
> MICROSOFT   AVIS

1. Snap! Crackle! Pop!
2. Where's the beef?
3. We try harder.
4. I can't believe I ate the whole thing!
5. Look, Mom—no cavities!
6. Fly the friendly skies …
7. I've fallen and I can't get up!
8. I must be in the front row!
9. Good to the last drop.
10. It keeps going and going and going …

Q49. Do you call them blinds or shades? Lightning bugs or fireflies? Match up these other words that vary from one region to the next:

1. can
2. cooler
3. skillet
4. bucket
5. faucet
6. turnpike
7. plug
8. davenport
9. veranda
10. tune up

a. interstate
b. hydrant
c. spigot
d. porch
e. couch
f. lube job
g. pail
h. fountain
i. commode
j. frying pan

Q50. Now look over these old American traditions. Simply add a word:

1. Folks sat down to eat, bowed their heads, and said …
2. Kids did chores, so that they could earn their …
3. Local policemen could be seen walking their …
4. When a baby was born, the proud father handed out …
5. After supper, couples would sit outside on the …
6. Ladies would attract gentlemen by dropping their …
7. Boy Scouts helped little old ladies across the …
8. Kids had to mind their manners and respect their …
9. Teenage schoolgirls would allow boys to carry their …
10. Citizens would gather to discuss concerns at the town …

Answers

Q47. 1. *Football* 2. *60* 3. game 4. Johnny 5. *Sesame*
6. Los Angeles 7. *Addams* 8. *Candid Camera* 9. *Zone*
10. *Meet*

Q48. 1. Rice Krispies 2. Wendy's 3. Avis 4. Alka-Seltzer 5. Crest
6. United 7. Life Call Med Alert 8. Miller 9. Maxwell House
10. Energizer

Q49. 1. i 2. h 3. j 4. g 5. c 6. a 7. b 8. e 9. d 10. f

Q50. 1. grace 2. allowance 3. beat 4. cigars 5. porch (swing)
6. handkerchief 7. street 8. elders 9. books 10. hall

Give yourself 1 point for every correct answer:

BORN IN THE U.S.A.

• Some of the soap operas of T.V.'s golden age included *Peyton Place, One Life to Live, All My Children, Days of Our Lives, General Hospital,* and *As the World Turns.*

A LITTLE HISTORY

- The **Twilight Zone** television series was a collection of various tales ranging from the tragic to the comedic, which always kept the viewer guessing because of their surprise endings. The popular show ran from 1959 to 1964, and was created by **Rod Serling** who played the host. Serling also wrote most of the episodes.
- W. K. Kellogg began his cereal-making career in the 1890s, when he helped his brother, Dr. J. H. Kellogg, by creating meals for the patients of the Battle Creek Sanitarium in Michigan. In 1906, Kellogg began to mass-produce and market **Kellogg's Toasted Corn Flakes**, and later added **Kellogg's Rice Krispies** in 1928.
- In 1956, **Crest** toothpaste, featuring a stannous fluoride compound patented by three Indiana University researchers, hit the national market. Royalties helped build the future Oral Health Research Institute in Indianapolis, and the toothpaste's advertising campaign (**Look, Mom—no cavities**) is embedded in American popular culture today.

SAY IT RIGHT

- Here are more examples of all-American word-trimming:

    I'm tired of my RV. I'd love a new Beemer or Jag, but I can only afford a V-dub or Chevy. But for tonight, the limo we rented is a Rolls!

- One little word goes a long way in our language. Can you figure **out** the pattern below?

    Stick out, ask out, buy out, try out, take out, string out, pull out, put out, cop out, clean out, sell out, turn out, point out, eat out, walk out, leave out, help out, look out, run out, shoot out, hang out, watch out, dry out, sit out, throw out, close out, rent out, stay out, hand out, and then **fall out!!**

Follow in her
footsteps

ON YOUR OWN

1. *Do you **dunk** your donuts?*
2. *Why would you **tie a string around your finger**?*
3. *Have you ever supported the **Special Olympics**?*
4. *Where do you put your hand when you say the **Pledge**?*

WORDS OF WISDOM

"Television has brought back murder in the home—where it belongs."

Alfred Hitchcock

WHAT'S MY SCORE?

TOTAL CORRECT: _____

TOTAL POSSIBLE: ___406___

FINAL NOTE

So how'd you do? Did you answer most of the questions correctly and quickly? Obviously you did better in certain areas and time periods than in others. Roughly, we would say that if you answered correctly eight times out every ten, you may congratulate yourself as being a red-blooded, all-American reader. Five to seven out of ten means that you are firmly grounded on this land, although probably you are either quite young or were born abroad. Time will get you to the top. Less than five means that you are more than likely still sharing the languages and cultures of your country of origin rather than those of the United States.

Storm in a teacup

For those of you who are competitive *and* ambitious, you may find the absolute total score. Simply add **all** your points from **all** seven chapters.

WHAT'S MY TOTAL SCORE?

GRAND TOTAL CORRECT: _____

GRAND TOTAL POSSIBLE: ____2807____

You know that the list of all-American English is endless. Therefore, if you recall or learn a classic word or expression that is not included here, feel free to write it on the lines below:

_____

_____

_____

_____

_____

_____

_____

_____

_____

_____

_____

Crossword Puzzle Answers

Crossword Puzzle 1

Crossword Puzzle 2

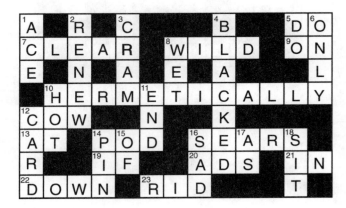

Crossword Puzzle 3

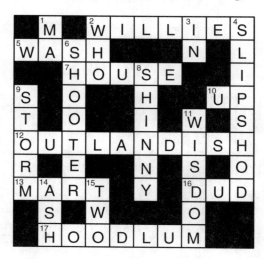

Crossword Puzzle 4

Crossword Puzzle 5

Crossword Puzzle 6

Crossword Puzzle 7

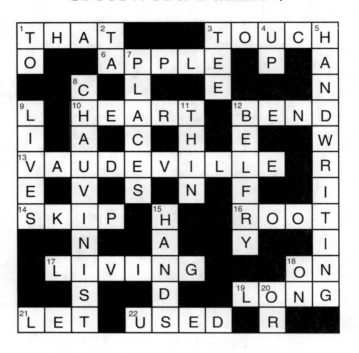

GRAMMAR GRAMMAR & MORE GRAMMAR

For ESL courses . . . for remedial English courses . . . for standard instruction in English grammar and usage on all levels from elementary through college . . . Barron's has what you're looking for!

501 English Verbs, *Thomas R. Beyer, Jr. Ph.D.* An analysis of English verb construction precedes 501 regular and irregular verbs presented alphabetically, one per page, each set up in table form showing indicative, imperative, and subjunctive moods in all tenses.
ISBN 0-7641-0304-0, paper, 552 pp., $14.95, Can$19.95

Grammar in Plain English, 3rd Ed., *H. Diamond and P. Dutwin* Basic rules grammar and examples clearly presented, with exercises that reflect GED test standards.
ISBN 0-8120-9648-7, paper, 304 pp., $14.95, Can$21.95

Painless Grammar, *Rebecca Elliott, Ph.D.* Focused mainly toward middle-school students, this book takes a light, often humorous approach to teaching grammar and usage.
ISBN 0-8120-9781-5, paper, 224 pp., $8.95, Can$11.95

1001 Pitfalls in English Grammar, 3rd Ed., *V.F. Hopper and R.P. Craig* Covers those trouble spots, including use of negative forms, noun and verb agreement, much more.
ISBN 0-8120-3719-7, paper, 352 pp., $12.95, Can$18.95

A Dictionary of American Idioms, 4th Ed., *A. Makkai, M. Boatner, and J. Gates* More than 5,000 American idioms and slang expressions are defined and explained.
ISBN 0-7641-1982-6, paper, 480 pp., $14.95, Can$21.95

A Dictionary of Homophones, *Leslie Presson, M.A.* Presented are more than 600 sets of words that sound alike but are spelled differently, with different meanings.
ISBN 0-7641-0168-4, paper, 224 pp., $10.95, Can$15.95

All prices are in U.S. and Canadian dollars and subject to change without notice. Order from your bookstore—or directly from Barron's by adding 18% for shipping and handling (minimum charge $5.95). N. Y. State, New Jersey, Michigan, and California residents add sales tax to total after shipping and handling.

Barron's Educational Series, Inc.
250 Wireless Blvd.
Hauppauge, NY 11788
Order toll-free: 1-800-645-3476
Order by fax: 1-631-434-3217

In Canada:
Georgetown Book Warehouse
4 Armstrong Ave., Georgetown, Ont. L7G4R9
Canadian orders: 1-800-247-7160
Fax in Canada: 1-800-887-1594

(#90) R 10/04

BARRON'S

Visit us at www.barronseduc.com